PIDGIN EYE

PIDGIN
EYE

by
Joe Balaz

an **ala** press offering
Honolulu, Hawai‘i

ala

means "basket" and "nest" in the Chamorro language and "path,"
"fragrance," and "to rise up" in the Hawaiian language. As such, we chose to
honor our press with the name Ala because of our belief that
literature has the power to carry, nurture, guide, beautify, and awaken.
We publish a diverse range of styles in poetry, fiction, creative
non-fiction, drama, graphic novels, and children's books by writers who trace
their genealogies to the native peoples of "Polynesia," "Micronesia," and
"Melanesia." If you are interested in submitting a book-length
manuscript, please inquire via email, nalani.mcdougall@gmail.com.

Co-founders: Brandy Nālani McDougall & Dr. Craig Santos Perez

Other ala press books can be purchased on Amazon.com
Nafanua, edited by Dan Taulapapa McMullin (2010)
Penny for Our Thoughts, by Kamehameha Students (2011)
Matamai2:Intersecting Knowledge across the Diaspora, by Pacific Islander
    Studies Students, edited by Kerri Ann Borja-Navarro, Richard Benigno
    Cantora and Andrew Fatilua Tunai Tuala (2012)
Afakasi Speaks, by Grace Teuila Evelyn Taylor (2013)
Squid Out of Water, by Daren Kamali (2014)
passages inbetween (is)lands, by Audrey Brown-Pereira (2014)
Sourcing Siapo, by Penina Ava Taesali (2016)
Full Broken Bloom, by Grace Teulia Taylor (2017)
Home(is)lands: New Art and Writing from Guåhan & Hawai'i (2018)

Visit our website at www.alapress.org

Contents

DA HISTORY OF PIGEON

Like different kine words
da world wuz full of different kine birds

yellow birds, blue birds, red birds, lovebirds,
and den came da pigeon.

Da history of da word pigeon is li'dis—

Wen da French speaking Normans
wen conquer England in da year 1066

dey wen bring along wit dem da word pigeon
foa da type of bird it wuz.

Da resident Anglo-Saxons used da word dove
or d-u-f-e, as dey used to spell 'um,
to mean da same bird.

It just so happened
dat terms in Norman-French
wen blend wit Old English sentence structure
to form wat we now know as Middle English.

In da process da French word
became da one dat referred to da pigeon
as food.

Today in England if you look foa dem
you can still find recipes foa pigeon pie.

Food foa taught, aah?

Even back den da word pigeon
wen blend wit pigeon foa get some moa pigeon.

So nowadays get pigeon by da zoo,
get pigeon on da beach,
get pigeon in town,
get pigeon in coups,

and no mattah wat anybody try do
dey kannot get rid of pigeon.

I guess wit such wun wide blue sky
everyting deserves to fly.

TINKING ABSTRACT

Da neurons are surging
on da spider network

omnipresent in da dome

so flash me some neon
and some wild kalakoa

and watch everyting
flow on its own.

I stay tinking abstract

so no give me
wun funny kine look

cause you not going find it
in wun puzzling stare—

open your mind
and start tinking da kine

and den you going see
someting dere.

Fluid and captivating
in wun free form notion

from wun idea to da canvas
in wun visual magic potion.

Imua! Banzai!

da signals are sparking
in da brain

cause everyting is revealed
by simply viewing

wit nutting to explain.

IN DA SAME PLACE

Eh, wats da mattah wit you, brah?
You no can see I get da same kine eyes as you?

I see da same tings,
my mouth talk da same,
my heart in da same place.

So wat if I no like use good English—
Baddah you?

Just because you li'dat
tinking you bettah den anybody else

try listen to dis poem dat I wen write
"head in da clouds."

Da sea is so beautiful
calm and serene
like waves of taught
on wun dreamah's dream.

Da day is so lovely
undah cleah blue skies
as visions of nature
dance in my eyes.

It's anadah beautiful day
in Hawai'i Nei.
To da guys dat no care
dat may sound so cliché.

But it is
wun beautiful day
in Hawai'i Nei
so no let da beauty
just pass away.

Da sun has wun passion
foa da land and da sea
I feel its golden warmth
shining down on me.

At leisure on da sand
I space out in dreams
and enjoy da magic
of island scenes.

It's anadah beautiful day
in Hawai'i Nei.
To da guys dat no care
dat may sound so cliché.

But it is
wun beautiful day
in Hawai'i Nei
so no let da beauty
just pass away.

Kinnah nice, aah?
I tink so too.

I hope you like 'um
so I can show
da snobs at da university

and da guys
in dose fancy poetry clubs

I see da same tings,
my mouth talk da same,
my heart in da same place.

VERBAL KINE JAZZ

See da old man

wit da cho cho lips
and da rat bite on his head—

Aisoos! Mongoose!
da fighting chicken wen lose

and now da buggah is dead.

Pluck all da feathers
trow 'um in da pot

everybody like kaukau

poho loosah
in da ring anyway

so now we going make luau.

Everybody dance
everybody sing

everybody jan ken po

no need fight
foa dessert tonight

cause we all get kulolo.

Look at da moon
up in da sky

just like wun big fish eye

sit on da ground
wit wun fat opu

and no even wonder why.

New kine story
same kine smell

everybody understand

all mix up
like wun big fruit cup

heah in da hula-hula land.

So now local lingo
is just like wun jingle

hololoho good fun razz

kissing da ear
making everyting clear

living in da verbal kine jazz.

ANYTING YOU KILL YOU GADDAH EAT

Wen I wuz wun small kid
my faddah told me

anyting you kill you gaddah eat.

You shoot da dove
wit da BB gun

you gaddah eat 'um.

You speah da small manini
at da beach

you gaddah eat 'um.

You help your maddah
kill da chicken in da backyard

you gaddah eat 'um.

Whoa, brah,

tinking back to small kid time
and da small kid games I used to play

aftah I heard dat
no moa I kill flies wit wun rubbah band.

RONNIE BUMBOOCHA

He wuz always fat
as long as I can remembah

and it wuzn't because of his glands—

da buggah just loved to eat.

In da cafeteria
he wuz in heaven

and he would pig out all da time.

He wuz da only guy I evah knew
dat ate two lunches on wun regular basis

followed by wun ice cream sickle
and three candy bars.

His focus on his grinds

wuz like wun hungry dog
chomping down on wun bone.

You could paint his nose blue
and chop off one of his legs

and he wouldn't even notice.

His size attracted Mr. Kim dough.

He wuz wun assistant coach
foa da jayvee football team

wen he wuzn't teaching social studies.

He talked Ronnie
into trying out foa da team.

I tink he wuz just looking foa bodies.

Wen da new potential offensive lineman
came out of da locker room
foa da first time

it wuz really someting—

he looked like wun beach ball
wit wun guava foa his head.

Dey tried to teach Ronnie
how to block.

He kept tripping ovah his own feet.

Da only good play he made
wuz wen he wen accidently slip

and pancake his own quarterback.

He quit aftah one week of futility
and Mr. Kim wuzn't disappointed.

We wen joke latah
dat maybe Ronnie
should join da diving team

cause he would be good foa sure.

All he had to do
wuz step off of da board

and da buggah would make
wun unreal cannonball.

DA SKATEBORDAHS
OF KE ALANUI LANE

Eh, we into skateboards, brah!
To da max!

Wheah we live we known as
"Da Ke Alanui Lane Gang,"
and sometimes we go riding
wit maybe eight or ten guys.

All of us dress da same too, brah,
wit baseball caps, tennis shoes, and socks,
and da kine ovahsized shirts and shorts
dat look like dey belong to Shaquille O'Neal.

Dats da style, brah.
Da clothes stay loose so can jam moa bettah.
And brah, wen we jam we do anykine.

We make spinning wheelies,
we flip da board and land back on top,
and we like to hop da sidewalk curbs.
We even hop da low cement wall at da park.

But da time Matthew
wen make wun move
by da bus stop, cuz,
dat wuzn't too cool.

Mrs. Delasantos wuz sitting on wun bench
waiting foa da bus foa go store.

Matt wen come and carang wun jump
off of wun nearby flower bed wall.

She wuz all piss off wit da noise
and wuz even moa mad

because da doves dat she wuz feeding
wen scattah, brah!

She wen give Matthew da stink eye
but he wen only laugh.

Yeah, dat wuz kinnah dumb,
but nutting compared to wen Dean
wen make his suicide run.

He wen start on Ki'eki'e Street,
da road above Ke Alanui,

and wuz coming down da hill
in his crouching surfah stance
full speed, brah!

But at da bottom turning into Ke Alanui
had some loose gravel.

Dean wen slide big time
and he wen crash
through da neighbah's wooden fence

knocking down almost wun whole row
of tomato plants.

Old man Hashimoto, our neighbah,

wuz working in his garden
and he went ballistic, brah!

He wuz screaming like wun psycho
so Dean wen get up, jump on his board,
and he wen dig down da sidewalk.

Old man Hashimoto
wen run by his broken fence,

pick up one of da loose tomatoes
dat wuz lying on da ground,

and he wen fly 'um, brah,
hitting Dean right in da back of his head.

Unreal aim
foa wun old man, aah?

Anyway, da blow wen make Dean
lose his balance again

and he wen crash one moa time
into wun parked Toyota down da street.

Unbelievable, brah!
Dat day Dean wen eat it
from two Japanees!

Talk about eating it, brah,
dats wat happened to Ikaika too.

He wuz hiding behind
da mock orange hedge by his house

wen his sistah's boyfriend and her
wen pull out of da driveway
foa go cruise in his car.

Ikaika wen grab da back bumpah
wen dey wuzn't looking

and he wuz making
like wun caboose, brah,

wen da boyfriend
wen burn rubbah around da corner
foa impress his sistah.

Because of dat
Ikaika wen bazooka out
on his skateboard

and he wen explode into da trash cans
by Choy Leong Market.

Eh, I wen score wun choice board

aftah his angry faddah
wen fling 'um down da road

before he wen take Ikaika to da hospital
foa fix his broken collarbone.

I only had to repair da front wheels.

Yeah, heah on Ke Alanui we have good fun
but sometimes we do stupid tings too.

Wen I stay jamming out on da road
wit my skateboard

my oldah braddah just look at me,
shake his head,
and den he smile.

He tell me,

"Eh, brah,
wen you discover chicks

you not going need dat board
foa hang ten
and da ride going be righteous."

Him and his girlfriend
dey like foa weah tight jeans
wen dey walk down da street togettah.

Her hand stay stuck inside
one of his back pockets
and his arm
stay wrapped around her waist.

But you know wat, brah,
wen I stay stroking da asphalt
on my skateboard
I kannot imagine any bettah ride den dat—

And besides,
I still dunno wat he talking about.

JUNIOR LIKE BE WUN RASTAH

Wit da colors of wun traffic light

dreadlocks
and da beat of Jamaica

Junior like be wun Rastah.

He got da fevah, brah,
full on delirious and getting moa nuts.

Nowadays, he always weah da kine
red, yellow, and green tee shirts

wit Ethiopian lions on top.

And he talk
wit wun funny kine accent too, brah.

You tink he stay Kingston
instead of Kaneohe.

Plus, he only listen reggae

and he get bumpah stickahs of Bob Marley
all ovah his low ridah truck.

His new ways wen even trow off
da coach of our canoe club, brah,

because of wat happened da adah day.

You know our club, aah?
Na Mano Melemele? Da Yellow Sharks?

Our symbol is da yellow outriggah
on da side of da canoe.

Aftah practice
Junior wen buss out two cans of spray paint

wit da crazy idea

foa paint da front part of da outriggah red
and da back part green.

He said da added colors
would give da canoe cosmic energy
in da watah

and make us go moa fast.

By da time
da coach wen find out about da paint job

Junior wuz in da showah

listening to his latest cd
dat wuz blasting real loud
from da locker room.

Wen da coach wen storm in
and catch him dancing to da beat
of one of da most radical reggae songs, brah,

right deah he wen realize
dat Junior wuz beyond lolo.

On da showah hook
had wun red, yellow, and green towel.

And den da coach wen look down
and spak da hair between Junior's legs—

Brah, wuz all dreads.

LAPA POI BOY

Dat romantic guy, Lapa,
had all da moves

so smooth like wun ili'ili stone.
I can just hear him now—

Your eyes
are like two mahina moons
and you nevah have maka piapia.

   Oh, Lapa.

And your smile
look like squares of haupia
so sweet all in wun row.

   Oh, Lapa,
   you so poetic, you.

And your lips
are so wet and inviting
like Sandy's on wun choice day.

   Oh, Lapa,
   no make li'dat.

And your breasts
are like two Mauna Kea-s
in Decembah
I like foa climb and ski.

Oh, Lapa,
you so da kine.

And your adah lips
must be like opihi, babe.
Wen da buggah stuck on da rock
even da crashing waves no can separate.

Oh, Lapa,
you so nasty
I going tell.

And your dress
is like wun candy wrappah.
Wen I hemo da back
da stuff is so—

Eh! Maile Girl!
Wat he telling you?!

About da moons,
da haupia, and da opihi?!

He wen tell your friends,
Lokelani and Judy,
da same tings last week!

Yeah,
Lapa had all da moves.

Escaping down da street
running away from wun angry maddah
and all da stones and punches

dat Maile Girl wen trow at him

no wonder
he would become known latah
as one of da most slippery
and sly talking playboys evah—

Lapa had lots of practice.

BOOMAH WILLIAMS

Da buggah sure can run wit dat pigskin
even dough it's really made of cow.

Boomah Williams
is wun pretty good running back.

Da only ting is

da knots in his head
stay just as thick as his powerful legs—

moa dumb den wun box of coconuts
is putting it mildly.

But foa now
he's da bull of da campus

and he gets his pick

of all of da girls dat stay ogling
around him.

Scholastics is wun lazy mystery
to Boomah.

He's relying on his good looks

and breakaway speed
in da open field.

Some college recruiters
stay looking at him.

Dey wondering
about his grades dough.

Boomah is tinking

dat he going skate through
to da next level

just like he did in high school.

He's already dreaming
of da new uniform.

Even dough some universities

try to accommodate guys
wit easy passable courses

it just might be too much
foa somebody dat no like give any real effort.

I can imagine him
struggling wit such subjects

as Finger Painting 101
and Farm Animal Identification.

Boomah sure can run fast

but not fast enough
to make da intellectual cut.

Da sad ting heah

is dat he not even trying
foa expand his brain

but da buggah going find out
da hard way.

Looks like
you no can change da stripes

on wun manini.

SHE'S GOT DREAM BOYS IN DA ATTIC

She's got dream boys in da attic
and some new intentions too—

looks like da kid
going be hard to handle.

Pull in da parental reigns

and watch dat filly's hooves
go crashing through da wall

as she breaks free

and goes running into da night
crazed and rebellious.

Hoping dat she wuz still wun virgin
has just been canceled

and now da wish is
dat she no get pregnant.

But let's not get too one-sided
and overly critical

cause somebody is partnering
wit somebody.

All da palomino colts
are sowing dere wild oats

in plain view
of wun double standard

so let's tag dose studs too
wit some equal responsibility.

It's wun powerful
two-way issue

dat good old court and spark

and everyone
wants to be prancing in da pasture.

Look at da spirit
in dose intense eyes

da flowing mane
and da flared nostrils.

She's kicking up her legs
like wun bronco

and dere's no corral in sight

cause she's got dream boys in da attic
and real ones in da basement.

LESSON IN SCIENCE

Da round yellow eye
wuz as big as wun dinner plate

in da head of wun huge alien serpent—

Looks like we are not alone.

Da legion of hairless monkeys back home
are in foa wun surprise

cause we just got wun jolt
of cosmic commonality

from da rest of da universe.

I taught it wuz amazing
wen I saw da Great Red Spot up close

but now my heartbeat
has raced to da finish line

as da answer
to da momentous question of adah life

is now swimming around me in circles.

Inside my luminous suit
beneath wun foreign sea

I move in strange currents
and view wat humankind has dreamed about.

Wats even moa fascinating

is dat it's right heah
in our own backyard

twirling around da same sun.

Europa
has offered up its ocean secrets

and I'm basking in da glow
of sudden insight.

It's as startling
as two eyelids opening

to da pouring in of daylight.

Discovery is wheah you find it

and da instructor
standing deah before me

is going to attest to dat.

He wacked my desk
wit wun ruler

to get my attention.

I wuzn't really napping—

I wuz just taking
his possible life on adah planets lecture

further den he could even imagine.

COULD HAVE BEEN CATHOLIC

I could have been Catholic
but I wound up
Seventh-day Adventist instead

until I had da choice
to be watevah I wanted to be.

It's all because of wun priest
and dose two nuns
dat came walking down da street

in da family history story
dat wuz told to me.

It wuz old-fashioned kine times
not like it is today.

My faddah wuz wun sergeant
in da U.S. Army.

He met my maddah
and dey eventually got wun house in Wahiawa

wen dey became husband and wife.

Dey wuz newlyweds
but dey nevah get married
in da Catholic church.

Da priest dat knew my faddah found out
and he decided to make wun unfortunate visit.

He walked up da stairs
looked inside da window

and shouted wun announcement into da house
aftah yelling out my faddah's name.

*"You are living in sin,
and you are going to Hell!"*

My faddah came to da door
and den he angrily answered,

*"I'm not going to Hell, Father,
but you are going down these stairs!"*

In da scuffle wit wun shove

da priest
went stumbling down da steps

in front of da two stunned nuns.

Latah on

my faddah
wen talk to wun bishop in Honolulu

who said dat da priest
had no right to do wat he did.

Howevah, da holy man did say

dat it would be bettah
if my faddah wuz remarried
in da Catholic church.

Dere wuzn't any agreement on dat dough

cause my faddah made anadah
life changing move
and he decided to become wun Protestant.

Dats why
by da time I came along

I had to observe da Sabbath
from Friday evening to Saturday night

and I couldn't go play outside
or watch television.

Bible school every Saturday morning
and church service afterwards

wit all da stuffy elders shaking my hand
wen I left to go home.

Thank God
wen I reached fourteen

my faddah gave me da choice
if I wanted to go to church or not.

He must have mellowed out
wen he got oldah.

If it wuzn't foa dat aggressive priest
pushing his weight around

I could have been Catholic.

*"Hail Mary
full of grace,"*

I would have been praying
at da altar.

Most likely dough

even da faith of da Rosary
wouldn't have made wun difference—

I tink I still would have bolted
wen I had da chance.

HOLLYWOOD WUZ IN TOWN

It wuz wun special day
in Wahiawa

standing on da sidewalk
watching everyting happen.

Hollywood wuz in town
making wun movie on location

and da old wooden buildings
on Cane Street

wuz going be on da big screen.

It wuz pretty exciting

to see da director
and all da technicians

create someting
before your eyes.

In da middle of da road
wun guy wuz flat on his back

looking through wun large camera
dat wuz pointed to da sky.

He wuz lying down
behind wun driver

on wun go-kart contraption.

Da two guys wuz in position
and ready foa shoot

so da director wen shout
foa quiet on da set.

Dis wuz right aftah
his assistant dat wuz next to him

wen finish talking on wun radio receiver.

He wen coordinate
some kine of coming event

wit wun pilot dat wuz on his way.

Us kids wuz wondering
wat wuz going on

and den you could hear
wun distant drone

dat wuz getting louder
and louder.

Suddenly

da go-kart wen go racing down da street
wit da camera rolling

at da exact same time

wun formation of Zeroes
came roaring ovahhead!

Da planes sounded
like dey wuz just above da rooftops

and da moment wuz electric!

Wow!

Dats wat dey must have looked like
on December 7th

and da director got it all on film!

Wen da movie
came out latah

me and my friends
wen watch it at da theater

looking foa da Japanee fighters
attacking our hometown.

In dat respect
it wuz kinnah funny and anticlimactic

cause Cane Street wuz on da screen
foa only wun couple of seconds

showing some people
running into wun building.

If you wen blink your eyes
you would've missed it.

Sometimes so much is left

on wun film company's
cutting room floor.

Not everyting
can make da cinematic view.

It's just like real life

wit da scenes you keep
and da ones you let go.

KIMOTHERAPY

Eh, you heard da news?
Daniel in bad shape.

He wen get Kimotherapy.

Yeah, I know,
kinnah sad, but—

Good foa him!
Da buggah deserves it.

Freaking rip-off artist
probably lippin to wun nurse right now

but no need feel sorry foa him, brah.
Da moa he suffah da bettah.

I tell you, cuz,
bad luck wen grab him by da neck.

Danny Boy taught he wuz happening
wen he wen steal dat surfboard
from dat car down Sunset.

I heard he wuz all mouth
aftah he wen try 'um out at Ehukai.

But wen he wen swipe dat board
from dat parked car next to dat beach house

too bad he nevah see da small haole kid
dat wuz looking through da hibiscus hedge.

And moa worse
too bad Daniel nevah know
dat da kid's oldah braddah

wen just finish surfing
wit da guys dat wuz driving da car.

You know dem, aah?

Alika, Roland, and Kimo,
da guys from Hauula.

Dey wen stop by Sunset
to visit dere haole friend
foa talk story little while.

Wen da small kid
wen run into da house
foa tell dem wat happened

dey wen all make it out in time
to see Daniel's blue sedan
turning da corner down da road

wit Kimo's board
sticking outtah da window.

So now Daniel stay hospital
wit wun broken face—

Wen dey wen finally catch him
one week latah

he wen get dirty licking

cause braddah Kimo
wen give 'um— therapy!

NO MAKE LI'DAT

First time on Molokai

I drive to da west shore.
I like see wat Oahu look like.

I not sure of da direction
so I ask wun teenage couple on da beach,

*"Eh, howzit, can see Oahu
from heah or wat?"*

Braddah tell me
as he begins to point,

"Oh, kinnah cloudy today,

*but if wuz cleah
Oahu would be
right about deah— "*

Just den
his girlfriend wen interrupt

and point somewheah else,

*"Oh, deah! Stay ovah deah!
See da mountain?"*

—but no moa nutting.

I turn to walk back down da beach
and behind me I hear braddah say to her,

"Wat you make li'dat foa?"

And dey call Molokai
"Da Friendly Isle."

WITOUT EVEN TINKING

New scientific research
says dat humans can sniff out

moa den 1 trillion different kine scents.

Maybe dat explains da abilities
of Haunani Rose Dela Cruz.

Da study went on to say
dat humans even have wun nose foa danger.

Wen dey wen ask women
foa sniff sweat dat dey wen perspire earlier
undah uncomfortable conditions

dey made funny kine facial expressions
like dey wuz adjusting dere present emotions

to da scents dat dey wen smell.

No wonder Haunani Rose
always give da stink eye

to all da guys at work
trying to hit her up foa wun date—

she got wun powerful nose.

Da scientific paper also said

dat da fear or da disgust response
to wun smell
can occur inside da nose

before da signal
even reaches da brain

allowing foa wun ultra swift reaction.

Dats why wen da braddahs cut da cheese
Haunani Rose always disappears

before da full hurricane hits.

Foa wun woman
wit wun sensitive nose

it can be very important
in lovemaking and choosing wun mate too

because of all da pheromones
and stuff li'dat.

Dats why all da despicable guys at work
no moa chance wit Haunani Rose—

witout even tinking
she knows how to smell wun rat.

CATCH DA BONE

Blood rushes through da body
like liquid shock waves

and da rhythm of limbs
stride to wun steady beat

in catching da bone.

Heightened appetite
enrages da hunger

and da mouth
foams wit anticipation

of teeth and tongue in oral bliss.

Fastah and fastah
on bouncing legs

wun sleek bullet responds
to each magnificent stroke.

Drive 'um!
Drive 'um!
Drive 'um, brah!

Into da air
wit wun mighty pelvic thrust!—

And all da adults applaud
and da kids let out wun cheer

as Ilio da pit bull
runs across da lawn

to catch da bone.

NEVAH WUN SOFTBALL

I wen read wun article
about prostate health, aah,

so I wen tell my friend, Donald,
because we both stay ovah forty,

"Eh, maybe we should go doctor
foa check it out."

He tell me,

"Prostate?! Dat has someting to do
wit your ding-ding, aah?
No tanks, braddah!
Nutting's wrong wit mine!
I just make believe my wife
is wun canoe—
I paddle all night long!"

And I tell 'um,

"I not talking about dat!
I talking about your prostate!
Da stuff stay inside
next to your bladdah, li'dat.
Wen we get oldah
sometimes da ting come big
and even turn into cancer, brah!"

Donald wen look at me again
and saw dat I wuz serious

so he wen say,

"Eh, cool down, cool down.
Heah, I make wun saying foa you,
make you feel bettah—"

"May your prostate always stay
da size of wun walnut
and nevah turn into wun softball."

Den he wen just laugh.

Da only ting I could say to dat wuz,

"Eh, Donald—
I can live wit dat."

NAMOKUEHA
Da Four Islands

Way down inside

I always knew why I had wun affinity
wit da Land of da Rising Sun

and now several anthropologists
like confirm da reason wit wun new theory.

Dey say dat wen some
of da ancient Polynesians
wen begin to migrate out into da Pacific

dey wen start further up north in Asia
den previously believed

wit da taught dat dey wen pass through Japan
and wuz deah way before da Japanees.

Eh, I could've told 'um dat

cause all dat info stay stuck
deep in my collective memory, brah.

I found all dat out wen I wen meditate.

Somehow wit relaxed breathing
and witout drugs

I wen realize dat I could tune in

to my ancestral heritage
foa contemplate da long look back.

All at once
like coming through wun tunnel
everyting wen look different

and I could see cherry blossoms falling
wit beautiful Mt. Ke'oke'o in da distance—

Namokueha
da four islands.

Dats da original name foa Japan, brah.

It used to be wun nice place
but cuz, wen da wintah wen come
wuz too damn cold!

Dat wuz one of da reasons
we wen hele on!

Plus, our chief, Maka Nui,
who wuz also our best navigatah

and who wuzn't too crazy
about da cold weadah eidah

wen figgah dat if we could find
dis place off of da Asian continent
den maybe get adah places out deah too!

Bettah yet
maybe da adah places stay moa warm.

Wat amazing vision cause Maka wuz right.

You heard of da Bermuda Triangle, aah?

Well, Maka Nui and da Polynesian ohana
wen embark on wat became known as
"Da Great Pacific Boomerang."

First, he wen sail us from Namokueha
into da far unknown

all da way to wun place
he wen name aftah his faddah—

Hawai'i, brah,
wheah warm weadah and wun nice suntan
wuz happily discovered.

Den, high on success,
Maka wen take us on wun unbelievable dig
from Hawai'i to wun island off da coast
of wat is now known as Chile.

He wen name da place
aftah his cousin on his maddah's side, Rapa,
who wuz wun unreal stonecuttah.

From deah, confident in his moves,
Maka wen head south from Rapa Nui

and wen find on da horizon wun new land
undah wun long white cloud.

He wen stick out his tongue in excitement
and shouted, "Aotearoa!"

unknowingly naming da place right on da spot.

Next, wit da quest of moa islands in his eyes,

Maka wen sail up north and came upon Tahiti
named foa his maddah

wheah da first bottles
of Tahitian beer wuz brewed
to honor da occasion.

And finally, from Tahiti,
using his magnificent navigational skills

Maka Nui wen sail da remaining ohana
back to Hawai'i

thus completing
"Da Great Pacific Boomerang."

And all because
Namokueha wuz too cold.

Absolutely incredible!
History is truly fascinating.

And sometimes now knowing all of dis
I have taughts from da heart

of one day going back to Namokueha
to trace da steps of my ancestors
and see wheah Maka Nui once lived.

Wit da rising sun rising
I would find myself surrounded by trees

wheah I would sit in silence
undah da reach of blooming branches.

As da day brightened to wun softah blue
I would observe just like wun Buddha

da peaceful beauty of cherry blossoms
in da old country—

But den again
sentimentality aside

maybe visiting Namokueha today
would be about as interesting

as going to Pearl City
foa da very same reason—

dat "Little Tokyo" town
got too many Japanees!

PORTAGEE JOKES

"It's kinnah funny
to see wun Portagee in wun Volvo—

honk da horn
and it sounds
like wun grandmaddah goose."

Kenrock Medeiros
made up dat lame joke in his head

driving on da freeway to da airport.

"Vovo— Tutu— You get it?"
he asked wun imaginary audience.

Shaking his head
he laughed at his stale humor
and said to himself,

"Aaah, nevahmind..."

He wuz in wun good mood
and acting silly
cause he wuz on his way to Portugal.

Kenrock went to St. Louis High School
and den to Villanova.

He latah became wun fast track CEO
in da financial world
and made buku kine bucks.

Wun Portagee joke he is not

and if you taught
only Pakes wuz good wit money

take wun good look
at Kenrock Medeiros.

His wife wen leave earlier
and she wuz already in Lisbon

waiting foa him to arrive.

Dey wuz going check out
da Madeira Islands

wheah dere relatives
and malasadas came from.

Wen Kenrock boarded da plane

he sat down in his seat
and looked down da aisle
towards da pilot in da cockpit.

He taught of anadah lame joke.

"How many Portagees does it take
to fly wun airplane?

None—

wen you can easily pay
adah people to do it."

Kenrock Medeiros
stretched out his legs in first class

and headed to his vacation

screwing in wun giant light bulb
in his head by himself

while smiling and illuminating
his big, bright world.

CHLORINE JONES

She calls herself
Chlorine Jones.

Her faddah wanted her
to be wun champion swimmer
but she can't even dog paddle.

She can pole dance dough

and she doesn't need wun bathing suit
to look Olympic.

It makes me suspect
dat da promo show biz story

about her daddy's wishes
to be known in swimming pools
around da world

might be somewat exaggerated.

Observing her moves

I have to admit
dat she's in great shape.

It's quite impressive
to do wun squat split
and slowly kiss da dance floor.

Wat control!

She is so close
you can almost touch her.

It gets wun immediate rise
and wun standing ovation
from da entire male audience.

I guess she likes performing
undah da bright lights.

She seems to be smiling
in da magenta neon glow.

Chlorine Jones—

She is swimming
in everyone's mind right now.

The whole club
would love to take da plunge
and dive down deep.

It's always wun new world's record
every time she takes da stage.

KULIOUOU KLEPTO

She taught
she had all da right moves

but da hidden camera
saw tings differently.

Da young woman from Kuliouou
got some nice bracelets in da end dough—

Wen she wuz arrested

dose silver handcuffs behind her back
fit really good.

It's wun unusual way to go shopping
foa panties and halter tops.

Even da police wuz amazed
at how many stolen items

she could conceal all ovah her body.

Too bad she's not as sly
as her braddah.

He's ripping off cars foa wun living
and he hasn't been caught yet.

Da buggah is wun real pro
at popping out door locks

and digging out wit stuff

wen da tourists leave dere valuables
in dere rented vehicles.

Unlike his sistah
he must be da brains in da family

because dere faddah stay in prison
and dere maddah is on probation.

Kuliouou klepto

sitting in wun police car
looking out da window—

good ting she no moa kids.

LOMILOMI DA BUGGAH

Kennedy Chang

wuz named
aftah wun famous president.

Like his namesake
he wuz wun good talker

and he could dish out da charisma.

Dere wuz someting about him dough
dat wuz kinnah sneaky.

His old high school friend Marcus
suspected it early on

and he had him down pat.

"I'll tell you about Kennedy—

*Ask not wat da buggah
can do foa you*

*but foa wat you can do
foa da buggah.*

*Dat Pake
could massage da scales off of wun dragon.*

Shifty too, brah."

Granted he wuz wun intelligent dude
and he did quite well at Iolani

but you wonder
why his moral compass

wuzn't inherited from his parents.

Dey wen work hard
to put him on solid ground

and now he stay sinking
in his own quicksand.

Aftah college
and his degree in economics

you would have taught
dat he would harness his potential

and work hard foa da legal tender.

Dats why

wen he wuz caught
in wun investment scam

preying on old people
and emptying out dere savings

all da relatives wen freak.

Da golden boy
trimmed in red foa good luck

wen turn out to be
wun common thief.

Wen his old friend Marcus
wen find out

all he could say wuz—

*"You give Kennedy wun opening
and he going lomilomi da buggah*

*and all da rules
going fly out da window."*

Dats pretty much wat he did

and dats how
da fortune cookie wen crumble.

SMILE FOA DA PICTURE

Let's hear it
foa anadah candidate

to be considered
foa da *Stupid Crooks Hall of Fame.*

Da possible inductee

wen post
wun selfie photo of himself

holding wun large amount of cash
on social media.

Dat wen help da authorities
to quickly zero in on him.

Da money
dat he wuz showing off wit

wuz part of $45,000 he wen steal
in two armed bank robberies.

Wun informant told da investigators
dat da crook wen spend some of da cash

on wun old Corvette
and wun root canal.

Da television news

focused on da work
dat wuz done on his tooth

and da viewing audience
taught it wuz kinnah amusing.

It wuzn't too funny foa da thief
wen he wuz arrested dough.

Most likely he wuzn't smiling eidah

wen dey wen sentence him
to 18 years in prison.

Tings really going change foa him now.

He going have free food
free uniform

and free room and board.

To top it all off
da buggah going have free dental.

LENNY DA LOOSAH

Lenny worked
foa wun plant rental company

da kine business dat take care
of plants in da hotels.

To his co-workahs dat made fun of him
he wuz known as
"da mental from plant rental."

—not too much happening foa brains.

Sometimes dough
he could be funny in his stupidness.

Like da time some of da guys
wuz talking about "poontang."

Lenny taught dat
dat wuz da capital of North Korea.

Talk about dense.
He wuz tinking geography
but as foa da real subject mattah, poontang,
forget it—

Da closest he evah came to dat
wuz getting intimate wit wun bar of soap
in da bathtub.

So it wuzn't too unusual
wen he made friends wit Victor
anadah workah
wit wun low pilot light.

But at least Victor
wuz little bit moa togettah.

He had his own small apartment
and broken down car

while Lenny still lived wit his parents
and caught da bus to work.

Da two of dem started to do
all different kine tings

but as to how Victor wen convince Lenny
foa go Vegas wit him
nobody knows.

Dat wuz da first time
dat Lenny wuz even on wun airplane.

Sad story dough.
Two crazy dummies
ready to trow away dere minimum wage.

Well, if anyting,
you could say
dey did it foa da experience.

So dere dey wuz
in da great state of Nevada
learning how quickly money can go.

Victor wen blow his whole wad of cash
in half-an-hour

and because of dat
he wuz all bum out wit his beer
sitting at da bar.

And Lenny
like da bright technician he wuz

wuz playing wun long shot progressive machine
dropping dollahs in wun frenzy
da same way he eat sunflowah seeds.

Wit only two bucks left
in wun couple of minutes
he wuz going to be wearing
da same sorry expression as Victor.

But sometimes life
can do da strangest tings.

Sometimes you can fling
your trow net
and catch da most fish
you evah caught wit one trow!

Sometimes you can go hunting
and your dogs going corner

da biggest mountain pig
you evah saw!

Sometimes you can go trolling
and hook wun marlin
dat you swear
wuz biggah den da whole damn boat!

But dis, braddah,
wuzn't one of dose times.

Aftah Lenny's second-to-da-last dollah
wen slide into dat machine
it wuz even bettah—

1 million, 800 and fifty thousand dollahs!

Da buggah wen hit!

And somewheah in da sky
Lady Luck wuz dancing around
and smiling like wun upside down rainbow!

Lenny da loosah, brah.

He stay driving around town
in wun brand new Lexus!

Remembah poontang?

He didn't know
wat it wuz

but now suddenly

got plenty kine wahines
knocking at his door.

GAMBLE IN DA JUNGLE

Get wun grip and leap, baby,
and swing like Tarzan through da trees.

Five will get you ten
wun wild creature not going leave you hanging.

Wish foa three cherries
and wun big jackpot

cause it's all wun adventure
in da risky romance play

wen serendipitous chance
is mixed wit emotions.

Ride dat passionate tiger
and place wun wager on da thrill.

Nevahmind da claws
hidden in da cards.

Change partners if you must
just like slot machines

and look at how dat great ape stares at you
wit two eyes spinning like roulette wheels.

Dere's wun whole stack of chips
in da sparkle of desire.

Pull it in or pay it out
as all da monkeys start grabbing da vines.

Ace or joker on da top of da deck.
Somebody new is spying you through da leaves.

It's eidah predator or prey

so get anadah grip and leap, baby,
and answer all da tom-toms in your heart.

BABOOZE WIT WUN KAZOO

I'm just wun babooze
wit wun kazoo

and I played it
like it wuz Gabriel's trumpet.

Wen I blew dat milestone note

someting wen happen
and someting wen end.

I used to play
wun cool saxophone
foa her soul and mine

but now
flower to wilting flower

I'm simply buzzing
like wun dying bee

on my vibrating plastic toy.

Oscillating dissolution
like wun dark remembrance

is singing on da membrane.

I don't like losing
and I don't like being lonely

while da walls around me
are playing air violins

but dere it is.

I'm just wun babooze
wit wun kazoo

humming on da mouthpiece
da revelation of wun fool.

PORCUPINE MOON

Cupid's evil twin
is shooting poison arrows
and laughing uncontrollably

hitting da bull's-eye
ovah and ovah again.

If only human reason and forgiveness
had clipped dose wings

and sent dat little bastard
spiraling into wun dive

to strangle in da twisting free fall
of his own bow.

If only dat romance
nevah go bad.

If only da golden rings
nevah lose dere meaning.

If only da bond
nevah break.

If only da moon
wuz made of clay

and Cupid's evil twin
wen fire all of his poison arrows
towards dat heavenly body

instead of into fragile hearts.

If only dat wuz da case

dat lunar ball out deah
would be wun loving savior to all

and it would shine
like wun round porcupine

bristling light
in da smooth dark night.

3 MOA DOLLAHS TO MY ELEPHANT

3 pigs
3 blind mice
3 stooges

"3 moa dollahs to my elephant."

Da pachyderm line
is da wish I make

wen I hand ovah my money.

I got it from my nephew—

he wanted to sponsor wun elephant
in wun animal reserve.

Foa 50 bucks
he could contribute to its care

so he began to do
all da odd jobs
dat little boys do.

"3 moa dollahs to my elephant,"
is wat he said

wen he proposed
to rake leaves in da backyard.

I laughed
and dose words stuck

becoming da mantra to my own dream.

"3 moa dollars to my elephant,"
is wat I say to myself

wen I give my weekly bet
to da cashier

intoxicated wit gambling desire.

Like wun pig
wanting it all

like wun blind mouse
reaching in da dark

like wun stooge
believing it will happen

I buy wun lottery ticket

wit jackpot odds
of 1 in 250 million.

"3 moa dollahs to my elephant,"

pink and fat
flying up deah in da sky.

ELVIS LIVES IN MAUNAWILI

Elvis came out of da bushes
on da walking trail

in full regalia
in his dazzling white jumpsuit.

He asked me foa wun light
but I told him I no smoke

so he took off his dark glasses
and he looked me in da eye.

I saw pinwheels and sparks
and heard funny kine noise

and all da birds, and da clouds,
and da trail wen disappear.

Next ting I knew
I wuz in da HIC

in wun good seat
looking at da stage

watching *Aloha from Hawaii*

beaming on wun satellite
to da rest of da world.

In da early 70s
dat Presley concert wuz wun big event.

Da music wuz entertaining
da show wuz choreographed
and da program wuz wun hit—

but den I wen hear wun loud thud.

I found myself
on da walking trail again

looking down at wun coconut
right in front of me

dat just fell from wun tree.

Strange kine taughts
wuz going through my head.

Maybe I get sunstroke
cause I no smoke pakalolo.

Just den da coconut on da ground
wen split open

and out jumped Elvis!

He wuz only da size
of wun mongoose now

but he smiled
and ran back into da bushes.

Lucky foa him
no moa any dogs around

cause dey could have bit off his head.

Even foa me
dis trail not dat safe—

dats wat dey tell me anyway
wen I can remembah.

Elvis is wun nice guy dough
if you get to know him.

Wen he came back to regular size
we wen talk story little while

and he told me he likes it in Maunawili
bettah den Graceland.

Sometimes wen I look at his face
he get wun aura around him

and my head get all fuzzy
like I got wun migraine.

I don't know it right now
but my family stay looking foa me.

I wen walk outtah da house
wen my granddaughter wuz doing laundry.

Dey told da cops I had Alzheimer's.

Everyting is cool dough
and I not going worry

cause da King of Rock 'n' Roll
wen just sing one of my favorite songs

dat wuz written by Kui Lee—

"I'll Remember You."

I tink he wen sing dat song
at da HIC concert too

but now I kinnah forget.

Hard to know sometimes
wen you walk by yourself

wen your hair stay all gray
and you wonder wheah you stay.

Good ting I get Elvis
foa keep me company.

DEY LIKE BACHI HER MERCEDES

Carolyn Keiko Nakayama
wen hook wun big one

wen she wen marry Roger Sullivan.

He had ambition
and wun family tradition to live up to—

His ancestors
became rich in da land grab

wen Queen Liliuokalani wuz kicked to da curb.

Da young couple met at Punahou
and became sweethearts.

It got even sweeter
aftah Roger wen graduate from college

and started wun online company.

Da business took off

and eventually he wen sell it
at wun outrageous profit.

Carolyn just loves
da new house in Kahala.

Hard to believe dat she grew up as wun local
cause she look and act like wun Katonk.

Maybe dose years of living in Marin
before her and Roger came back to da islands

wen solidify her standing

as wun ultra example
of wun haolefied Japanee.

Some of her cousins
would kinnah agree—

Dey like bachi her Mercedes.

Looks like da bad vibes wen really flow
wen Carolyn made it known

dat wun branch of relatives
dat still spoke Pidgin

wuz wun embarrassment to her.

At da baby luau
foa Colten James Ichiro Nakayama

dere's one aunty
dat not going be kissing his cheeks.

It seems dat Princess Carolyn
no like hang out wit da serfs.

Bettah yet

cause plenty anxious tongues
stay waiting foa talk to her

sharp and ready
like wun guillotine.

SHE STAY ALL ANGRY

She stay all angry
telling me I driving her crazy.

Excuse me foa living

but I just trying to find
anadah good game on TV.

"Eh, look!

*Da Eagles are playing in da snow
in Philadelphia.*

*Amazing how dose people
live in da wintah ovah deah."*

She grabbed da remote
and turned off da power—

"You already watched wun game!

*I taught we wuz going shopping?!
You always do dis kine stuff to me!"*

Give me wun break.

I bet she no even realize
dat da running back in dis next game

just needs 38 moa yards
to go ovah 2000 yards in wun season.

Dats not wun easy ting foa do
and now I'm going to miss it.

"Football, football!
You only tink about football!

Wat about me?!

Wen wuz da last time
you took me to wun movie anyway?!"

Come to tink of it
I don't really know

but dats not important right now.

I gaddah calm her down
and take her to da store

cause wen she stay all angry
she turns into wun maniac.

It's not my fault

dat men can only focus
on one ting at one time

so I hope she appreciates da effort.

Aftah we got to da store
I walked around wit her

but wen she wuz looking
at some furniture

I disappeared around da corner
to da electronics department.

"You tink dese chairs
are worth da price or wat?—"

She wuz talking to air
cause I wuzn't deah.

If I taught she wuz angry before
I just took it to anadah level

cause wen she found me standing
in front of wun big flat TV screen

in da demonstration show area

her face wen turn red
like wun tomato.

All I could say wuz—

"Eh, how you like dat?!

Dat running back
made ovah 2000 yards

*and it's still snowing
in Philadelphia!"*

PAKALOLO PIRATES

Da dead dove

wuz tied to da top
of wun tall stick

wit wun small nail
stuck through its eyes—

somebody
wuz sending wun message

not to walk down
dat side trail again.

Andrew got all paranoid

as if he wuz looking
at wun skull and crossbones.

He started squawking
like wun parrot

tinking dat somebody
wuz going see dem
and get dere revenge.

Keoni had to calm him down.

Only three weeks ago
wen dey wuz hiking

dey wen score some choice buds

wen dey came across
wun pakalolo patch
in da mountains

in da same place
dat dey wuz standing right now—

It wuz like dey had wun treasure map.

X marked da spot
of da hiding place in da bushes

so Andrew and Keoni
came back to get some moa.

Not wun good idea
foa buckaroos to do

if you don't know who you dealing wit.

Somebody out deah
like make dem walk da plank.

Andrew and Keoni
took da dead bird as wun hint

and dey wen dig out

cause ripping off
adah people's plants twice

can be wun rough and risky business.

Moa bettah chicken out
den get all buss up

cause dat booty and plunder
not going be worth it

if dere okoles
get kicked to da moon.

KAHUKU CORN SALSA

Manu P. Gouveia swears
by his Kahuku Corn Salsa—

*"Broke da mouth
and hemo da brain,"*

as he would often say.

*"Good wit beer
and moa beer,"*

wuz da mantra
as he passed da bowl around

while he and da boys
dipped dere chips
and watched da latest sports event.

UH football
losing by 30 points
in da 3rd quarter—

So wat?
Get Kahuku Corn Salsa.

Bully pigging out
moa den usual.

Kawika forgetting
wat his first name is.

Henry disappearing
into da backyard

and talking to wun banana tree
as if it wuz his ex-wife—

Kahuku Corn Salsa
taking full effect.

Da secret
is in da preparation:

––30 ears fresh corn
––10 cups cherry tomatoes
––5 cups Maui Sweet Onion
––40 tablespoons minced fresh Maui Wowee
––20 tablespoons minced Acapulco Gold
––2 liters vodka
––and humungous amounts of Hawaiian salt.

Kahuku Corn Salsa—

breakfast, lunch, and dinner
of champions

and of Leonard
driving down da street

witout his car
or his clothes on.

SOMETING STAY IN DA WINGS

Weird?
You tink Robert is weird?

Not even close.

Weird is molding tofu
into da shape of wun vagina

and tinking about tings
you can do wit it.

Go ask Henry about dat.

But dats anadah story
cause we talking about Robert.

Braddah stay forming new priorities
if you nevah notice.

If he had to spend six months alone
at wun research station in Antarctica

he could do it wit no sweat.

So now you tinking he weird
or maybe turning gay

cause he nevah like check out da chick
dat you wuz trying to fix him up wit.

And no worry

I not going tell anybody
dats your cousin.

It would help dough
if she got her teeth fixed.

But if you ask me
I no tink she's Robert's type anyway.

He looking foa someting
all togettah different now.

I know you going have trouble
digesting dis taught

but Robert is just not interested
in one night fireworks anymoa.

He wants some consistency.
Look at him squinting at da morning sun—

just like he imagining somebody.

Dat blazing ball ovah da horizon
is rising into wun new day.

Someting stay in da wings
I can tell you dat.

Twenty bucks I bet you

Robert going see her pretty soon
wen he least expects it.

She going pop out of da periphery
and into da light

and braddah nevah going be da same again.

TOFU VAGINA

People go to places
dat dey no like admit to.

Maybe it just comes down
to stimulation.

Dats da driving force
of course

but as to how da mind
achieves dat pleasurable tingle

is anadah ting all togettah.

Kinky is wun subjective term.
It's like wun outpost on wun far border—

you can visit it
from time to time

and look out ovah da vast territory
of human carnal complexity.

Inventiveness
and innovation abounds

in da big organ
wit big ideas

being carried around
on top of wun willing body.

Henry flipped da light switch

and felt around in da dark
foa his molded soy creation

dat wuz lying on wun towel
on top of his mattress.

Call it flaky or bizzare
or out of touch weirdness—

In wun brain

dat doesn't even give it
wun second taught

it's just anadah avenue
to wun impulsive sensation.

BUMBYE BETTY

If wun pig could speak
it would be Bumbye Betty

rolling around in da mud
and talking stink about everybody.

Fat, obnoxious, and ugly,
and dose are her best qualities.

Yapping fifty miles in wun minute
she would make wun auctioneer
sound like he wuz talking in slow motion.

And her shining personality
brings tears to your eyes
like wun truck load of rotten onions.

Bumbye Betty—

Bitch wit wun capital B

da reason some men go insane
and da reason some women hate each adah.

Da center of all existence
exists in her selfish little pea brain.

She would make
wun rabid pit bull look charming.

Opinionated on everyting and anyting
as if she wuz da maddah of all creation

wen all she is doing

is passing gas
through both ends.

Bumbye Betty—

bad-tempered and malicious.

Bumbye she going put her foot in her mouth
and choke on it.

YOU NO CAN FAULT
WUN PALEONTOLOGIST

She got wun big head
like wun Torvosaurus

same kine appetite too.

I made wun run for it
and hid in da reeds
on da riverbank.

It wuz right next
to da coffee machine
and da watah coolah.

Parting da leaves
I looked down da aisle

and sprinted back to my desk—

I just missed her

but dere wuz huge teeth marks
all ovah da tabletop.

Dere wuz also wun email message
on my computer dat I read earlier—

it said,

"I will tear you to pieces
you blabbering little twerp!"

It's all in da science
of relationships I taught

and gossip really isn't gossip
in da information driven world.

I guess dis reasoning doesn't apply.

Wat she wuz saying wuz

wen wun female dino
wines and dines
it's nobody's business

even dough it may include
half of da studs
in da office tar pit.

I contend

dat you no can fault wun paleontologist
foa digging up bones.

I tell myself dis

knowing dat wun mouth
full of razor sharp daggers

is now on da rampage.

Excavating
her prehistoric secrets

is like inviting my extinction
to take place

at da upcoming company picnic.

LOUNGE LIZARD

Wit scales gleaming like sequins

her alluring tail slid by
taking his eyes wit her.

She disappeared mysteriously
into da crowd at *The Sand Bar*

wheah wun full house
altered dere senses

on cactus whiskey
and tumbleweed wine.

Her desert perfume
and oasis smile

removed him from his stool

to find out
wheah dis unusual female

had slipped off to.

He moved slowly
through da lively nightclub

as on stage
Billy Gecko and da Alligators

played dere style
of improvised jazz.

In passing wun nearby table

he ovahheard wun group
of loaded leathernecks argue

dat Tyrannosaurus rex
wuz no myth

and dat da fictional Godzilla
gave everyone wun bad name.

Unconcerned
wit such reptilian jive

he scanned
da entire ground floor

until he caught sight
of her again

sitting in wun far corner.

Dough she dressed like wun local
he recognized her as wun Tuatara

from dose outer islands
near Aotearoa.

Wit exotic spines
in da middle of her back

and wun well-developed
third eye

she wuz wun intriguing beauty.

As he walked ovah
he imagined her undressed

and he wuz just about
to deliver his line

wen wun huge Komodo dragon
in wun pinstripe suit

returned from da restroom.

Understandably discouraged

da lounge lizard simply slithered away
wit his pride deflated

as da Indonesian brute

sat down and kissed
dat fine feminine creature

in wun dream ending embrace.

HE WEN GO BUSS DA WINDOW

Da owner wen make like wun angel
talking to da reporter and da cops.

She wuz wun innocent victim
in da random and senseless crime.

Someting seems shady dough.

Wun neighbor walking his dog
wen witness da early morning attack—

how wun guy in wun hoodie
wen buss in da glass wit wun bat.

Den he wen escape
down da road in da dark.

Da popular Kapahulu restaurant's
front window

wuz in pieces on da ground
and da owner wuz all distraught

and seemingly wondering why
foa da cameras.

Da ting is maybe she already knew.

Kinnah odd dat her adah location
in Kapalama

wen suffah da exact kine damage too
on da very same morning.

Looks like da angry ninja
wen dish out wun double dose.

Dats wat happens

wen you charge
like wun bull on impulse.

Maybe da owner
wuz wearing wun red panty

dat only da vandal could see.

Both establishments
have da same name—

The Juicy Oyster.

Tongue and cheek
is laughing somewheah in da periphery.

Sigmund Freud's deep analysis
would appreciate dat play on words.

I can see him squeezing his lemon
on da half shell.

Da jilted lover wuz wun outfielder
foa Kaiser High School years ago

and he wen use his favorite bat
dat he wen keep aftah he wen graduate.

Unless da police
get lucky wit dere investigation

it looks like
nobody going get caught.

Da owner
is sweeping up da pieces now.

She's witholding
some vital information.

Love
or da lack of it

can be so mysterious.

HARLEY CARESS

I've nevah seen one of her movies

but I tink I know
wat da action scenes look like.

Her face is just as sexy
as da one on da DVD picture online.

Da only difference
is dat she's not wearing red lipstick

and she doesn't have
dat same frizzy hairdo.

I checked da photo out
on my computer

so I could identify her

cause my neighbor
in my apartment building

said dat she frequented
da corner pizzeria.

I don't even know
why I'm sitting heah

two tables away from her
watching her eat.

She no can see my quick glances

dat make me feel
like I'm looking through wun keyhole.

I swear

I'm not into pornographic pepperoni
or extra sleazy cheese

but I seem to be confusing myself
cause I kannot take my eyes off of her.

I imagine da room going dark

and da ghost of her cinematic exploits
materializing in frantic gyrations

on da wall behind her.

I don't tink I'm stalking—
I don't even know her.

Harley Caress
takes wun sip of her soft drink

as she finishes her slice.

Sliding da slender strap
of her purse ovah her shoulder

she stands
and den walks seductively

out da glass door.

I haven't felt dis way
since I wuz wun teenager

watching my first X-rated flick.

Risqué thrills
and tantalizing frills—

looks like
dis sexual fantasy ting

is wun lifetime gig.

HEAVENLY JOE

I just love dis stuff

and it's so good to eat
wen you get da munchies.

I get all wired too
aftah chomping down on dese grinds.

Wen I do my buggy dance
foa my honey

she spread her wings
and tink I funny

and fly away
before I can attack her tree.

She no like share
da experience

of both of us
chowing down togettah.

But I kannot help
being how I am

cause I like to work dat hole
and crawl inside

and get to da core
of da bean—

I not kidding
I got wun big appetite.

You might tink I'm wun pig
or even wun pest

but I'm just wun average
boring beetle

and everybody gaddah eat.

So sorry about da prices
going up in Kona

I know I stay cutting into da crop—

but maybe dose growers
ovah deah

should plant bananas
or someting else

cause all of dese coffee berries
are just everyday heaven to me.

TYPEWRITING MONKEYS

English is definitely
not dere first language.

Da theory goes

dat if you give
wun infinite numbah of primates

wun infinite numbah of typewriters

eventually da buggahs
going produce da works of Shakespeare.

Researchers at wun university
in England

wen put dat notion to da test.

In wun project

intended more as performance art
den scientific experiment

faculty and students

in da university's
Anthropology department

wen put wun computer

into da monkey enclosure
at wun nearby zoo.

Dey wen find out

dat six monkeys left alone
wit da machine foa one month

attacked da ting
and failed to produce wun single word.

Dey did have wun random coincidence
wit da letter S dough.

At first
da lead male got wun stone

and started bashing da hell
out of journalism's longtime tool.

Anadah ting
all of dem wuz interested in doing

wuz in defecating and urinating
all ovah da keyboard.

In da end da monkeys wen produce
five pages of text

composed primarily of da letter S.

As far as evolution goes

now we know
wheah certain media critics came from.

I DUNNO IF YOU WEN NOTICE

I dunno if you wen notice

but Marvin's cousin
no shave her armpits—

It's like talking to Chewbacca.

Too bad

cause she got wun good figure
and her face is kinnah cute

if you can get past
her hairy arms and legs.

Eh, everybody got dere quirks
physical and mental.

Looks like she wuz given
wun extra helping dough

of adah tings dat show up
wit further observation.

Foa instance

da way she eat
wuz wun trip in itself.

Aftah I first met her
at Marvin's house

wen she wen pop in
foa drop someting off

I wen invite her
to go get plate lunch wit me.

We went to da drive-in
around da corner

and I wen order us some stuff.

I only took couple of bites
from my chicken katsu

and she wen already scarf down
her whole plate of kalbi

inhaling all da food
like wun freaking vacuum cleaner.

Wen she saw da reaction
in my raised eyebrows

she wen explain

dat she grew up
wit five oldah braddahs

and dat she had to learn to eat fast.

As she continued talking

I saw dat she wuz really aggressive
wit wun toothpick to clean her teeth

not to mention latah

dat she wuz also
unconsciously playing

wit da long strands of hair
on her left forearm too.

Okay

I wuz tinking
of initially trying to get her in bed

I not going lie.

But now
I having wun second taught

wit all of dese red flags
flapping in da breeze.

Da male sex drive
is wun powerful ting

but it looks like reason
just flew back into da window.

CHAMELEON LAUGH

"Wun guy walks into wun bar
and asks wun person standing nearby,

Why does my nose hurt so much?

Da gym instructor tells 'um,

Next time duck down moa low."

Isaac dunno
if dat joke wuz evah told before

cause he made it up

just like da adah one
he wen share yesterday.

"Talk about bad timing—

dere's nutting worse
den choking on wun piece of aku poke

while playing wun game of charades."

He tinks he's wun comedian

wun messenger
of da chameleon laugh

dat makes fun
of da human condition.

Hard to know
if his taughts are original.

It seems highly possible

dat somebody somewheah
must have said 'um before.

Den again

Isaac did seem
to have wun sharp wit

so maybe dere's someting
to his authorship.

He wen demonstrate dat
wen we wuz playing chess

on wun outside tabletop
at Ala Moana Beach Park.

Wun passing tourist

wit wun tinge of smugness
in his voice

wen abruptly ask us
in front of his girlfriend—

*"Do you people
still live in grass shacks?"*

Witout hesitation Isaac wen say,

"Do you still live in wun log cabin?"

Da guy seemed to be kinnah startled

and den he wen slink away wit his partner
while giving wun slight stink eye

as if his put down intention
wuz exposed.

Isaac nevah care
about da reaction.

He wen just chuckle
and forcefully say,

*"Checkmate, brah,
and wun big aloha to you too."*

Den he wen smile
and look at me

as if he wuz on stage
wit wun microphone.

I wen just shake my head
and laugh

and den I wen tell him,

"Brah, now dat wuz funny."

URGENCY TEST

Dis is wun test
of da urgency broadcast system.

Right now
on every radio station

you stay hearing dis same test
all ovah Hawaii

including Papakolea.

Your safety demands
dat you learn wat foa do
in case of wun urgency.

Wit dis test
you going simultaneously hear

two different kine sirens
outside your window.

Da first one
going be wun loud continuous siren.

Dis is da attention alert signal.

In da case of wun real urgency
listen foa instructions on your radio

cause maybe wun tidal wave
or someting li'dat
stay coming.

Da second siren
is da attack warning signal.

Dis going be wun loud continuous
wailing sound

but I not talking about da sounds
dat whales make
wen dey stay mating off of Maui.

I talking about wun loud wailing sound

da same way Jimi Hendrix
used to wail on his guitar
in da old psychedelic days.

Wen you hear dis sound
dis is wun sign of enemy attack
so you suppose to run
and take cover.

But you know wat, brah,
if dis had been wun actual enemy attack

in my opinion
you can just kiss your okole goodbye!

Cause how you going run
from wun nuclear missile?

You evah seen
one of dose buggahs explode?

And wat if da enemy
wen fire moa den one
like maybe fifty or sixty?

Guarantee we going take gas!

And wat if had wun big earthquake
on da American continent
and California wen fall into da ocean?

Da tsunami dat going come
going be so huge
going cover all of da islands

and you surfahs
going have da ride of your life!

All da rest of us
bettah invest in scuba gear!

And wat if da sun wen just explode
and vaporize da whole solar system
into wun incredible cosmic cloud?

You going be tinking
too bad you nevah take
dat neighbah island trip!

And wat if da whole universe
wuz just sucked
into wun humungous black hole

and matter nevah mattah anymoa
cause nutting going really mattah?

If conscious reality nevah exist

you wouldn't have to choose
between saimin and pizza!

But wat if I only exaggerating?

And wat if da only disasters
are da small ones
dat happen everyday?

—like da high cost of housing
car insurance
or da price of food?

Wat if da local politicians sell out
and all da developers go berserk?

Wat if dey cut welfare
wat if moa people use drugs
and wat about violence on da streets?

Wat about aloha
wat about wun bettah lifestyle
and wat about beating up women
and child abuse?

Wat about me?
Wat about you?
Wat about us?
Wat about everyting
we trying foa do
in dis strange cultural stew?

We stay searching foa answers
hoping foa answers
we need some answers.

True or false
multiple choice
any good response will do

cause dis
is only wun test.

CHARLENE

Charlene
wun wahine wit wun glass eye

studied da bottom
of wun wooden poi bowl

placed in wun bathtub
to float just like wun boat.

Wun mysterious periscope
rising from wun giant menacing fish

appeared upon da scene.

Undahneath da surface
deeper den wun sigh

its huge body
lingered dangerously near da drain.

Wun torpedo laden scream
exploded in da depths

induced by Charlene

who wuz chanting
to da electric moon

stuck up on da ceiling.

Silver scales
wobbled like drunken sailors

and fell into da blue.

No can allow
to move da trip lever on da plunger

no can empty da ocean

no can reveal da dry porcelain ring
to someday be scrubbed clean.

Charlene
looked at all da ancestral lines

ingrained on da bottom of da round canoe
floating on da watah

and she saw her past and future.

Wun curious ear wuz listening

through wun empty glass
placed against da wall

and discovered
dat old songs wuz still being sung

echoing like sonar
off of da telling tiles.

REGARDING WAFFLES

Saluting amber fields of grain

begin wit 2 cups of flour

4 teaspoons
of baking powder

and 1 ½ teaspoons
of pillar of salt

taken from da outskirts
of da new Gomorrah.

Foa good measure

don't forget
da 2 tablespoons of sugar

in respect
to founding plantations everywheah.

Mix and sift
all of dese dry ingredients
in wun empty bowl

while exhibiting
wun thankful expression.

In honor of all assimilated cows
dat routinely chew dere cuds

add 1 ¾ cups of milk
½ cup of melted butter

and two well-beaten eggs
preferably from wun apathetic chicken.

Pour dis combined concoction
into wun blender

and whip at extremely high speed.

Aftah achieving
wun smooth and creamy consistency

plug in da waffle iron
which is uniformly indented

like da first lines
in all da paragraphs dat justify da recipe.

Wen it's hot enough

apply batter and bake to serve
wun heaping plate of crispy brown

impressed by wun bunch of squares.

UNCLE KAULANA GIVES WUN SPEECH

I want to get all of your attention today
foa wun very important issue
and dat issue is sovereignty!

And dis is da main ting I want to say about it—

Sovereignty is wun good ting
if we can just figure out wat it is.

I know wat you tinking
heah's anadah guy talking about sovereignty
but wat he going do foa me?

Da question is not wat I going do foa you
da question is wat you going do foa yourself!

No be wun babooze
and just sit on your okole
waiting foa everyone else
foa do someting.

Do it yourself!
Participate!

And I talking mainly about
all of you fair weadah Hawaiians.
You know who you are!

You like to go to da canoe race
and hula festivals

but wen come to da hard stuff
like Hawaiian politics
you about as brown as Snow White!

But dis is no fairy tale, people!
Cause we talking about wun movement
and dat movement is moving!

True
it's not always moving
in da same direction

but nevahdaless it is moving
and dat, my friends,
is bettah den nutting.

Nobody said it wuz going to be wun picnic.
You gaddah invest your time and energy!

Let me put it dis way.

Da sometimes heah
sometimes deah

back and forth feeling
dat you going get about sovereignty nowadays
is just like da stock market.

Sometimes da market stay up
sometimes da market stay down.

Sometimes you feel like wun bull
sometimes you feel like wun bear.

But as long as you stay willing
foa take wun risk and invest

ovah time you going score
and you going come out ahead.

And coming out ahead
is wat we all striving foa.

I know many of you out deah
are listening to me right now
and saying to yourself,

okay, Uncle, sovereignty,
but wat da stuff going look like?

You hear all dis talk
about different kine models.

Nation witin wun nation
state witin wun state

you don't know wat kine model
foa choose.

Nevahmind all of dat now!
Da idea is foa tink small
but at da same time, tink big!

Let me give you wun analogy, li'dat—

Da kine model we need
is like da kine model airplane

you used to make
wen you wuz wun kid.

(dats if you wuz wun boy. If you wuz wun
girl, well, you gaddah tink of anadah analogy).

But, anyway,

just like dat model airplane
you going patiently put
all of da pieces togettah.

And wen dat model airplane stay pau
you going hang 'um up on da ceiling.

And den you going make anadah one.
And your friend going make one.

And his friend going make one.
And his friend's friend going make one.

And before you know it
da whole ceiling going be full of airplanes

and we going have wun dynamic ceiling
instead of wun empty floor!

Hanging up deah in da sky
wun Hawaiian air force
foa support da ground troops!

Dats da kine of collective model you want!
And dats da kine of model we need!

If we could be in control
anyting is possible!
Believe it!
Hawai'i going be different!

We going grow taro instead of pineapples
and Hawaiian and Pidgin going be
da official languages of da land.

Tourists going be confined on tour buses
and dey not going be allowed out of Waikiki
witout wun visa.

You not going see dem anymoa on public buses

and I talking mainly about da Circle Island one
wheah dey take every available seat

making all da local people
stand up aftah work.

And da guys you love most,
da military,
going pay substantial rent
and dey going follow our rules.

All dere maneuvers
going be held in California

and wen dey stay in Hawai'i

aloha print going be mandatory
and incorporated into all of dere uniforms.

Changes like dese
are coming, people,
coming down da road
as fast as wun stolen Honda.

But you know

even wit all of dis new found optimism
and ideas about da future
we still get our critics

especially from dose people dat not Hawaiian
who came from da continent.

Dey like to say dat we kannot organize
and handle our own affairs.

Dis is wat I have to say about dose people—

No give me anymoa of dat
"crab in da bucket syndrome"

telling us Hawaiians
dat we just like crabs in wun bucket
always pulling ourselves down.

Crabs in wun bucket?
How's about lobsters in wun pot?!

Dats wat Congress in Washington is!

Everyday you get Democrats and Republicans
trying foa stab each adah in da back!

How's dat foa working togettah?!

It's wun struggle all da way around, people,
and it's not easy
but confrontation is necessary.

And sovereignty is someting
we all going have to deal wit,
today, tonight, or wenevah.

Wenevah, brah.

Wen Ewa makes wun move
Nanakuli and Waianae going follow.

Wen Ewa stands proud
Aiea and Waipahu going be right behind.

And da feeling going spread from Wahiawa
down to Waialua and Kahuku side

right around da island
to Kaneohe and Palolo.

And den da neighbah islands going join in

and sovereignty
going be on da television news
and in all da newspapers.

And as dis glorious movement
grows strongah and strongah

through all da rain, thundah, and whitewatah,
and watevah else dat may develop

I want all of you to remembah
watevah side of da fence you stay on

dat sovereignty means
nevah having to say you're sorry.

And as I finish my speech today
I know dat all of you going do
watevah you going do

but no be afraid to do
wat you tink is right.

Aloha nui loa
and eh,
malama da pono!

DA MAINLAND TO ME

Eh, howzit brah,
I heard you going mainland, aah?

No, I going to da continent.

Wat? I taught you going California
foa visit your braddah?

Dats right.

Den you going mainland, brah!

No, I going to da continent.

Wat you mean continent, brah?!
Da mainland is da mainland,
dats wheah you going, aah?!

Eh, like I told you,
dats da continent—

Hawai'i
is da mainland to me.

WHY DA POI STAY STALE

Wun speaker at da rally
can give you some reasons

as to why da poi stay stale
if you just listen.

He going start wit boots on da ground

and wun warship
wit its guns aimed at Iolani Palace.

Manifest destiny
works really well

wen you got da military might
to simply take wat you like.

Uncle Sammy
going crush you undah his feet

if you try resist.

Tecumseh, Crazy Horse,
and Geronimo,

can tell you all about dat.

Scars and slights forevah
is da unfortunate result.

Nowadays

da island natives in da streets
continue to protest foa dere rights.

Adah people look at dem
and tink dey all stay disillusioned.

Dats wat happens
wen da blanket of assimilation

settles in ovah time.

Da guy blowing wun conch shell
in front of wun defiant crowd

not going agree wit dat.

As long as da faithful
know dere history

you kannot kill da truth
of wat is wrong and wat is right.

SPLINTERED PADDLE

Wen da cop wen approach
da homeless guy in Chinatown

da man wen reach behind his back
and whip out wun canoe paddle.

Den he wen swing dat ting
and hit da officer in da head

knocking da buggah out right deah.

Latah on at da hospital

da emergency room staff
had to pull out all da splinters

before dey wen put in da stitches.

Dey also had to treat
wun broken arm

and wun bad knee sprain too

foa da adah cop dat wen fall
wen he wen try use his taser.

Da guy wit tattered pants
saw da move

so he wen reach down
and grab da pavement

to pull it up like wun carpet
undahneath da surprised officer's feet.

Moa police came racing
down da street

wit all da sirens blaring.

Da destitute guy
wen just laugh at all da commotion

and den he wen melt like wun phantom
into da sidewalk.

Wen da cop wen approach
da homeless guy in Chinatown again

it wuz déjà vu part two

but it wuz unlike da dream
da guy just had

aftah he wuz awakened from wun nap.

"You know,

you lucky I not going arrest you again
like I did last time,

so pick up your backpack and leave."

Da homeless guy
walked down da sidewalk and disappeared

just like da cop and da business owners
wanted him to.

MEGA PIG HUNTING

Eh, all you local pig hunters
we gaddah upgrade—

Rent wun tank from da National Guard
and blow da buggahs up on da ridge!

I telling you
in tight spots on wun trail

wun handy bazooka
is way moa bettah den wun pack of dogs.

If you like protect ferns
and put food on da table

we gaddah use military tactics, brah,
like dose combat veterans in Georgia

looking through dere thermal imaging scopes
to shoot wild pigs in da dark.

Blame it on Hernando de Soto

dat Spanish explorer
from da sixteenth century

wen some of his hogs wen escape
and dig out into da forest.

Now dose wild descendants
stay all ovah Southeast America

rooting up farms
and people's gardens.

In da Peach state
dey not fooling around—

dey hiring veterans
and sending in da infantry.

So eh,
all you local boys

get out da grenades
and da automatic weapons.

We gaddah ambush da buggahs
in wun coordinated blitzkrieg attack!

Mega pig hunting
island style—

recreation and pork chops
wit wun new and improved purpose.

NO MOA CHANCE

Foa Jeremy C. Higa
finding wun reason to be negative

wuz about as easy
as finding wun Mormon in Laie.

It wuzn't because
he wuz Okinawan eidah.

All dat stereotypical racism crap
wuz from his grandparents generation

wen da Japanees
looked down on da Okinawans

because dey taught dat dey wuz hairy
and intellectually inferior.

Jeremy wuz wun smart guy.

It wuz just unfortunate
dat he wuz wun "pessimist."

Imagine him at wun motivational seminar
sitting in da audience

listening to and commenting on
wun highly optimistic speaker—

*"Aah, waste time. Dat stupid stuff
not going work."*

—Jeremy C. Higa in wun nutshell.

It wuzn't like he had wun bad life growing up.

He wuz just wun moody guy
dat liked to be by himself.

And I no tink having wun common last name
had anyting to do wit his disposition—

Higa wuz just like *Smith* in Okinawan.

Dats just da way he wuz.

It's hard to know
how he got his prophet of doom complex.

He wen "blossom" little bit
wen he got oldah dough.

Wen he wen show up
foa wun pickup basketball game wit da guys

Ronald wen kid,

"Eh, heah comes Jeremy.

*I gaddah go
stick wun heroin needle in my arm*

and go jump off of wun bridge."

I just laughed
and I knew it wuzn't dat bad.

I would simply have to hear,

*"I no can dribble like you guys
and I kannot shoot dat good."*

Da negative monotone
wuz all too familiar.

Dats why it wuz amazing
wen Jeremy got married to Nalani.

Ronald wondered out loud,

*"How you figure dat?
He end up wit wun nice sweet girl."*

Nalani wuz positive too.
High energy to Jeremy's stick in da mud.

Dey wuz wun odd couple foa sure.

Her ting wuz she liked to go to Vegas.

It's unbelievable dat she got Jeremy
to go wit her on one of her junkets

even if she had to listen to—

"Aah, waste time. I not going win anyway."

Jeremy wuz true to form dough.
He lost at everyting he played.

I wen tease Nalani wen dey got back,

"Good ting he nevah hit wun jackpot.

He would have dropped dead from shock
and da buggah would have confirmed
his luck."

Nalani smiled
and joked as only wun married person could,

"I can only wish, Dennis.
Sometimes I can only wish."

WAY UP DEAH

Jared's maddah told him

dey wuzn't on da top
but dey wuzn't on da bottom eidah

cause dats wat da family genealogy wen say.

One of da given names on da list
dat wuz handed down to her

wuz translated to mean
"Da highest point of da mahiole."

Da average person in da village
not going have dat kine name.

So Jared wen find out
dat in old time Hawai'i

his family wuz from da chiefly class
right undah da king.

Dey wuz nobles in da social strata.

Dat wuz cool to know
if you into nostalgia

cause everyting stay different now.

Jared wuz high in da air
wen he wuz tinking about dat

on da side of wun building
in Honolulu.

Working wit wun squeegee
and swinging on wun rope

he kept adah people's view of paradise
nice and clean

washing windows
way up deah in da sky.

CHANTILLY LACE AND PEARLS

Kamuela Kim's
great-grandparents

wuz immigrant workers
in da sugarcane fields

but dat wuz da extent
of her humility.

She wuz da owner
of wun ritzy Honolulu restaurant

and her Cadillac
wuz painted bright ruby red.

The Tropical Summit
offered fine dining to patrons

and da profits
helped to keep Kamuela

dressed in da latest fashions.

She wuz affluent
in mind and body

wit her huge ego
and expensive jewelry.

Her nose wuz high in da air
and you could see her sitting dere

in da elegant dining room
of her fancy establishment.

She wuz just as regal

as da centerpiece
on da back wall

flanked by pastel paintings.

Up deah on wun pedestal

wuz wun beautiful porcelain doll
in wun exquisite Parisian gown

inside wun showcase.

Kamuela smiled
at da chic decor and ambiance

and took wun sip
from her glass of white wine.

She wuz light years away
from hanbok clothing

and very much at ease
wit Chantilly lace and pearls.

KILIMANJARO KALAMUNGAI

Wen Bernard Virgilio
became wun chef

nobody knew
he wuz going write

wun best selling cook book.

He became da toast of Kunia

and his show
Filipino New Style Cuisine

wuz very popular
on public television.

He always liked to cook

and good ting his family
had old recipes from his grandmaddah

cause Bernard
wen put 'um all to good use

by mixing in his own innovations.

His beef adobo
wuz ono delicious

and his puto rice cake
would just melt in your mouth.

But da best ting he made
wuz actually wun soup dish

called "Kilimanjaro Kalamungai."

People wuz confused dough
why he wen combine wun African name

wit his special soup
of kalamungai leaves.

Bernard wen explain

he wanted wun exotic name
foa his premier dish

and da famous mountain
represented wun high peak

and had wun catchy ring to it.

His good friend wen tell him
he should have called da soup

"Kaala Kalamungai"

cause dere wuz wun mountain
wit wun high peak

right deah in his own backyard
in Kunia

looking down at him.

Bernard wuz tinking big dough
like wun aspiring chef

way beyond Oahu
and ovah da sea—

He knew he wuz going global
wit his puto and adobo

and his crème de la crème
"Kilimanjaro Kalamungai."

BAMBOO HARVESTER

Bamboo Harvester
wuzn't wun panda in China

or wun man in da Philippines

cutting stalks
to make wun house.

Growing in popularity
instead of growing in da jungle

he wuz certainly good
at creating wun splash

cause you can get
pretty well known

wen you make people laugh.

He wuz silly
and outrageous

and you knew him
wen he became famous

wit his big eyes
looking at you.

Funny hay and wild oats
wit wun occasional crazy apple

helped to feed da absurdity.

Just like Lady Gaga
and Bruno Mars

his name wuz changed too
so he could be moa cool.

Ask his friend Wilbur
cause he knows all about it.

Mister revelation
going give you Ed in da shed.

*A horse is a horse
of course, of course—*

You can now start singing
da program's catchy song

anytime you like.

BOUNTY BOB

"Bounty Bob"
wuz wun really good pig hunter.

He wuz humble too
but he wuz wun man's man

tough and determined in da bush.

Everybody knew
who da king of da mountain wuz.

Bob took it all in stride
and he wuz always cool.

He went aftah da big male boars
out deah in da rain forest.

Dat wuz plenty of meat
to trow into wun freezer

foa family and friends.

Da whole hunting experience
wuz also wun spiritual trip to Bob

and he usually came back
wit wun good catch foa his kitchen table.

Dats why everybody
called him "Bounty Bob."

Wen he wen pull
into wun gas station

wit da latest big boar
in da back of his pickup truck

wun nearby tourist in wun rented car
wuz all excited

and she just had to take wun picture.

She went up to Bob
by da gas pump and told him

dat she could send him
wun copy of da photo

if he wanted one.

Da reply wuz classic—

*"No need wun picture.
I not into dat.*

*I already know
wat da buggah look like."*

"Bounty Bob"
hunter extraordinaire.

He gets his game on all levels.

BEYOND DA NINTH ISLAND

Plumeria Ikeda
wuz wun rambler and wun gambler.

Rather den just go Vegas
she kept on flying east

until she wen end up landing
by wun huge lake

dat looked as big as wun ocean.

In da city wit da *Rock and Roll Hall of Fame*
she suddenly found herself in Cleveland.

Wun old friend dat lived dere
wen recommend da downtown casino.

Plumeria wuz wun trailblazer

so she wen figure she go try someting new
to expand her expertise.

Her eclectic tastes
wuz just as unusual as her first name.

Da plumeria wuz wun flower
dat wuz most fragrant at night

in order to lure moths to pollinate it.

Da blossom had no nectar
and it simply fooled all da dumb bugs.

Plumeria's name sure wen fit her
wen she became wun player.

She had wun unrelenting focus
and wun very deceptive poker face.

Looks like da trip is paying off

cause Plumeria just walked out da door
wit eighty thousand extra dollahs.

Like wun new age pioneer
appearing out of da Pacific

she wen discover dat da Rust Belt
wuz just as profitable as da desert.

Plumeria Ikeda is coming on da scene
and taking off like wun rocket.

Her talent is purely on da up and up.

Looks like Atlantic City
going be next.

Aftah dat
she just might be flying ovah anadah ocean.

No be surprised
to see her eyes

checking out all da new opportunities
in Monte Carlo.

MANGO SAKAMOTO

Mango Sakamoto
wuz wun strange dude.

Da buggah
would hide in da bushes

and shoot at small animals
wit wun pellet gun.

He made Whitmore Village famous—

It had moa dead cats per acre
den any adah town on da island.

I would see him
everyday wen I came home from school

sitting on his parents porch
eating green mango and shoyu.

Dats how he got his nickname.

He wuz wun spooky kine guy
wen he gave you "da eye."

Good ting dey took dat stolen pellet gun
away from him.

Mango Sakamoto

wuz da same age as my oldah braddah
who just joined da Air Force

but he had wun baby kine mind.

He really liked *Kikaida*

dat red and blue android
from da Japanee program
dat ran on local TV.

He would pretend
dat he wuz dat sci-fi character

and he would jump and shout
and run around on da porch

like he wuz fighting monsters
or demons from da dark side.

Wen I wuz wun small kid
Mango wuz scary.

I wuz always afraid
dat he wuz going do someting bad to me.

Da buggah wuz mental

but you not supposed to say
stuff like dat.

I remembah da day
wen I came home from school

and saw all da cops standing around
wun ambulance down da street.

Dey had just brought up
wun dead body

from Kaukonahua Stream
down in da gulch.

Da investigators wen speculate
dat da person wen drown

aftah he wen wrap his own ankles
and wrists wit twine

and jumped
into da deep watah of da stream.

Da dead body wuz wearing
wun *Kikaida* tee shirt.

Mango Sakamoto—
Crazy, brah.

He wen take his own life.

Just tinking about it
gave me chicken skin.

Foa da longest time

I would walk pass
dat house wit da empty porch

and remembah dat nut case
and how afraid I used to be.

Dats how kids tink

wit tunnel vision
unable to see around da edges.

Mango Sakamoto—

Dere wuz probably
so much moa to his madness

but I wuz just too young
witout any empathy

to even see it.

DA NEXT BIG WATEVAH

Human nature no change
wen da time digits go by

so try dis battery-powered E-cig
wit induced vapors

and let me know wat you tink.

No moa any smoke or tar

but da ting stay infused wit nicotine
and it still has dat captivating hook.

Plenty people stay looking
foa da domino buzz

so dey can enhance
da wavelength.

So maybe you like some fake pot
dat new kine herbal incense

foa help you meditate
and medicate.

Put 'um on da stove
and call da kettle black

cause dat synthetic marijuana
still going make you loopy.

Oh, no!

We stay climbing da ladder now
slipping through da gateway.

Science marches on

and tink of all da goodies
dat stay coming in da future

to join old-fashioned
acid and ice

and all da adah
mind and body slammers.

Da next big watevah
coming down da road

going be selling euphoria
wit da latest escape.

Make sure you maintain
and keep your fingah on da brain

so you can avoid
da final megaton rush.

WEN DA DEVIL SMILES

I forgot
to pay attention to da road marker.

I forgot
visual images are transferable.

I forgot
dat I wuz going somewheah.

I forgot
every destination is just wun station.

I forgot
da silver lining is colorless in its dormancy.

I forgot
bad tings only happen wen da devil smiles.

I forgot
not to consume grass on da highway.

I forgot
da herd stampedes wit titanium hooves.

I forgot
objects get mangled on impact.

I forgot
wat da paramedic wuz telling me.

I forgot
spiraling like wun broken airplane.

I forgot
da feel of da emergency room.

I forgot
dat I wuzn't wun cloud.

I forgot
to take anadah breath.

I forgot
da pitchfork stuck in my throat.

I forgot
to open my eyes.

I forgot
to see da big red stop sign.

WAT WENDALL WEN DO

Sitting on wun frozen horse
going round and round

Wendall wen reach
foa wun golden ring

stuck in wun bull's nose.

Spinning like wun top

it wuz wun big time party
rushing to da moon

wit all da streaking stars
flying by.

Nirvana exists
and Wendall wen feel it

temporarily anyway.

He must have been dosing
wen da glass pipe wen break

wen da horns and hooves
wen trample him into da ground

and fling him from da merry-go-round.

Now Wendall get bugs
crawling undah his skin

and he's watching
little mouse people

fall out of da ceiling.

Da devil is in da retails

wen dey cook up
all of dose cold pills—

ovah da counter
and into da lab

wit wun mad scientist
pulling wun crystal rabbit

outtah wun hat.

Now because of dat
Wendall no moa teeth,

he no moa job,
he no moa house,

he no moa tent on da beach.

Wun batu ranger
is always in danger.

Pretty soon
he not going have wun heartbeat.

Wen dat finally comes around

pray dat Wendall sees
anadah golden ring

floating in da air
like wun halo.

TARANTULA BLUE

Out of da sighing pan and into da mire
wit head in hands
and wun dose of tarantula blue.

It's wun B movie in wun A+ world

wen wun monster rears its hairy legs
on da mind's silver screen.

From da burrow to da prey

madness struck in da cerebral cave
like wun hammer to wun anvil.

Da unseen audience gasps in unison

because da fangs wuzn't meant
foa wun super roach

laced wit tons of stimulant dynamite—

Popcorn puffs rain down on da carpet
like particles from wun nuclear fallout.

Da explosion wen create
wun new galaxy of stars
twirling ovahhead like wun whirlpool.

Somebody needs to get da usher.
Wun flashlight in da dark always helps.

While da theater spins in delirium

anadah menace is crawling up wun tree
to devour wun chick in wun bird nest.

Now dats wun bold idea

cause da move is wun high aspiration
foa wun addicted spider.

It's amazing wat you see in wun stupor
on da hell ride of wun drunken binge.

It's just as useful as today's torn ticket stub
foa next week's nostalgic black and white film.

FOA DA WONDERS OF DA UNIVERSE

You may have heard—

aliens are real
and dey can be contacted
through da U.S. Postal Service.

I'm looking inside wun dark mailbox

at shiny angelic faces
and strange metallic objects.

In da gleam of wun reflection

wun column of piled saucers
snakes its way into da clouds.

On da topmost plate
wun gathering of ants
are doing wun interstellar boogaloo.

Cosmic sugar
like Peruvian marching powder

can get da folic acid circulating
and cause all dose juiced up bugs

to head foa da da nearest black hole.

Leaping into wun prayer like wun lemming
everyone follows everyone else
in wun regimented litany.

Dere must be wun dead moth
somewheah near dat deflated space suit.

On my computer screen
I just got wun email—

it reveals dat magnesium
is da fuel dat runs dere vehicles.

Thank you so much Flash Gordon
foa your cryptic message.

If it wuzn't foa you

I would nevah have given up da saxophone
foa da wonders of da universe.

MESSAGE FROM DA COCKPIT

If da concept of being on top
or in da forefront captivates you

den bully foa you.

We simply adding
to wun ethereal cloud anyway.

I understand ego and drive
and da aerodynamics of ambition.

Keep in mind dough
dat everyone has wings

even wun little sparrow.

I can see plenty pilots
puffing out dere chests

and sputtering along
in dere vintage biplanes

attacking da blue
and taking it all so seriously.

Dats cool
cause da air up heah is fine

and wen I zip by
in my supersonic jet

I'll wave and wish dem well.

I'm not being judgmental
or even inferring dat I'm above it all.

I'm just flying.

Notice how dese continuous lines
in da form of vapor trails

are being left behind in da journey.

It's merely skywriting—
I hope you enjoy da read.

YOU NEED WUN ANGLE

You need wun angle
in dis big round world

full of deceitful jive
and unscrupulous characters.

Dey stay looking at you
in da smoke-filled parlor

trumped up on bourbon and beer.

Salivating like ruthless wolves
dere eyes and ears perk up

wen dey see you
next to da green baize

on da elevated rectangle.

Da predators are tinking
it's time foa wun feast

unaware dat dey going get fleeced.

Stroke dat cue stick
like wun spear

and send da money ball

into da side pocket

to rattle
and ring in da cash.

Hustling da hustlers
and stringing pelts on your shoulders

is bettah den getting striped naked
and kicked out into da street.

Congratulations

you look like you stay wearing
wun wild coat

wit all of dat harvested fur
hanging off of your bold frame.

It takes wun angle
in dis big round world

calculated and victorious
wit wun convincing geometry.

NO INSULT MY ANTENNAS

No insult my antennas
wit dat hypothetical could have been

as if it wuz wun whole different story
dat you can simply create.

Da way you see it

if it looks like wun coconut
smells like wun coconut
and tastes like wun coconut

den it could have been wun lychee.

Dat sounds like editing
and ovahlap to me

and I can do da same ting
just like you.

It could have been
wun donkey jumping ovah da moon.

It could have been
3 chickens instead of 3 pigs.

It could have been
wun lethal kumquat

instead of wun poison apple too.

It could have been lottah tings
but it wuzn't.

It simply wuz wat it wuz
and dats da way it is.

If you like speculate
on how tings could have been

den go make some new fairy tales
or nursery rhymes

and let your theories
drift off into lala-land.

None of your changing scenarios
or reinterpretations

going get any reception from me.

I no moa time
foa your altering agenda—

I got wun appointment wit da real.

WORTH NOTICING

Wen I took off
da cellophane wrapper

and cracked open
my fortune cookie

dere wuz no slip of paper
wit words of wisdom—

it must be some kine of sign.

Dat nevah happened before
cause I always got wun message

and now I wonder
if da whole order of my existence

wuz going be altered forevah.

It's like da butterfly effect
wen everyting influence everyting else.

No need to blame
da Chinese restaurant

cause all the cookies
wuz prepacked.

Wun absent-minded person

on wun bakery production line

forgot da insert

and now da ghost
of my missing aphorism

is floating aimlessly
into da ethers.

Dats wat it seems like anyway

wen you expect someting
and it doesn't come to be.

But dere could be moa to it

and da spirit of wun wise Hakuin
could be trying to reach me

in my profound
and pondering state.

If he is
he might have gotten through

cause I may have heard
da sound of one hand

wen I wen notice wun message
dat I nevah even see.

JANITORIAL MEDITATIONS

I stay all bright eye
in blue-collar radiance

mopping da floor
so da ting come sparkling clean.

Eh, look down
and see myself looking back up at me.

Just like wun mirror, brah.

Station to station enlightenment
seeing da scope of one's being and all dat jazz.

Maybe I should get wun orange robe
to go wit my rubbah work boots.

Den I can monk out wit da philosophy.

And check out dis brush
dat I twirl around da porcelain oval—

I achieve cleanliness
just like wun confession aftah wun prayer.

Disinfecting da bowl is okay.

Dat lemon fresh smell is so universal
but I prefer da scent of sandalwood incense.

I gaddah go outside da building next
and walk around da sidewalk
and da parking lot.

Wit every cigarette butt
I sweep into my dustpan

it makes me tink of all da smoke
dat wen spiral its way to heaven.

I spiral too, brah,
just as randomly wenevah I want to

cause now I stay speaking words of atonement
in da language of wun zephyr

floating ovah bones lying in wun desert
as if I wuz offering wun apology

to someting unrequited
and long since gone.

Take wun closah look
at dat skull in da sand being talked to.

It no can hear nutting.

Scorpions are crawling out of da sockets
cause dose romantic dreams
wen disappear years ago.

I taught I could comprehend
da missing wavelengths

but da visual remnants
dat I saw in da surrounding infinite grains

wuz just da tracks of wun sidewinder
slithering away.

Da buggah wen open its mouth
and show me its fangs

and I wen faintly hear myself muttering
wun litany of regrets.

Parched lips dat once felt kisses
formed all da sentences it wanted to

hoping to explain someting
to wun unreceptive skeleton.

Dats wat you call wun cathartic rumination
in trying to make amends aftah da fact

and look
dere's anadah cigarette butt in da desert

as wun circling hawk ovahhead is screeching
and ringing into my cellphone—

Da boss just told me
he wants me to watah da plants in da atrium.

His call
snatched me out of my meanderings.

So now I gaddah get wun hose
in da equipment shed.

Latah on
if dere's anadah fantasy brewing

dat hose just might turn into wun talking snake

winding around wun banana trunk
in wun tropical garden by da food court.

GUPPIES IN WUN GUPPY TANK

Da Big Honcho in da sky
is supplying all da fish food.

Da clean watah and da air too.

I know you no like hear dat
if you tink it's just wun fairy tale

but I stay leaning
towards wun omnipresent boss

wit enormous eyes
looking through da glass.

Dere's wun huge giant
walking around da living room

doing all different kine tings
in his own universe

while we stay swimming around
wit our tiny fish brains.

All da guys
wit da colorful tails

stay chasing
all da unwilling girls

and look at all da babies
hiding in da Java Fern.

Not to get
all metaphysical

but I see greater tings
in da bubbles and da H2O.

Guppies in wun guppy tank
like wun ant farm or wun zoo

wit someting unseen
and marvelous

actually looking aftah you.

WAT YOU GOING DO MANJU?

Jesus gets moa converts
and Buddha gets moa gongs

while da universe is spinning
and da angels sing dere songs

so wat you going do manju
wen da buggah comes aftah you?

Dat ageless figure behind your back
is wun heartless reaper, brah.

Look how he tears up dat calendar
and trows it into da air like confetti.

Some people freak out
and some people go insane

to see wun cloud of shredded days
falling inside dere brain.

It's wun big deal to know
dat your time is almost ovah.

So wat you going do manju
wen da buggah comes aftah you?

You no can run
you no can slide

you no can dodge da ending
on dis one way ride—

might as well just laugh
in his skeleton face.

Dat black robe and big sickle
not going baddah me

wen my mind turns off like wun TV.

So wat you going do manju
wen da buggah comes aftah you?

NOW YOU SEE WAT I SEE

a) keyboard waiting to respond
like wun machine gun.

b) white screen wide open
like wun willing virgin.

c) composer prepped and loaded
on anadah Moscow Mule.

Vamoose! Inspiration is on da loose!

Wun small mischievous guy
wit red skin and horns

stay whispering in my ear

while anadah little angelic guy on da adah side
is giving me haloed advice in wun tiny voice.

Ying and yang and da whole shebang
and wun gallery of selections to choose from.

I'll take wun shake, rattle, and roll,
and wun side order of improvised fries

to go along wit my expressive burger.

Look at how I arrange all da letters
on da flat polarized snow

da solid angular cloud

da wedding gown rectangle
dat stay in front of your eyes.

Let me add moa ballistic x, y, and z
to da typography

and see if it will compute.

Bang, bang, bang!

Read between da lines
as da silver bullets fly

and all da projectiles
get shot into your retinas.

Hocus pocus
it's suddenly in focus

and da narrative
is turned right side up in your brain—

Now you see wat I see.

SQUEEZED INTO SHAPE
LIKE WUN SAUSAGE

Spilling my coffee on da rug
is how I read wun Rorschach test in disgust.

No mattah how you live wit it
dere's always cause and effect in da stain.

Flying in wun nightmare
is da way I temporarily remove myself.

Notice how da wax and feathers fall away
wen I get closah to da sun.

Pulling into wun schoolyard
and not parking my tricycle in wun stall—

Maybe dis aversion to accountability
began wit my first expression wit wun crayon.

Removing white lint from my black sweater
is neither compulsive nor cathartic.

It's just dat da night doesn't seem complete
unless I eliminate all da tiny stars.

Denying myself of wun rainbow
is how I deal wit dat elusive pot of gold.

No sense tinking of riches
wen life only gives you shades of gray.

Walking on wun tightrope
witout wun balance pole

seems much easier to do
wen you notice dere's no safety net.

Desiring wun answer to wun demon
is like jumping into wun meat grinder.

Any longing will simply be processed
and squeezed into shape like wun sausage.

Lying down on wun shrink's leather couch
staring and mouthing words to da ceiling—

All da notations wit pen and pad
is nutting but expensive chicken scratching.

Looking into wun mirror
trying to make sense of it all—

Moa bettah to just accept it as is
and realize dat everyting is merely subjective.

OCEAN IN WUN CIRCUS TENT

It may be easier
to fill da whole ocean into wun circus tent

den to explain
why da acrobat does wat it does.

It's in da act and da nature of it
dat thrills da eyes and liberates da heart

in da joy of fascination.

You no can bottle da moment
and dere's no sense to analyze

da jumping dolphin in flight
high above da watah.

    Da pen moves
    across da page

    and da sea spray flies
    beneath da big top.

"Wat did you mean by dat?"
"At wat angle did it leave da watah?"
"Wat do dese passages mean?"
"Wat wuz da height of its apex?"

Da dolphin falls back into da sea
entering in wun rush

as oxygen bubbles float up
and burst upon da surface.

Yield to da muse
rather den da explanation

and da mind going fly wit fins
to da voice of da ringmaster.

MONGOOSE KILLAH

Watching in da grass
wit kaleidoscope vision

you rewrite da fable.

Aftah all
you stay up deah on wun pharaoh's crown

and da story is
watevah way you want it to be.

Scales are tensing
and rattling like warrior shields.

Dere's moa power in da belly plates
den you evah felt before.

Must be da vibrating energy
of da earth below.

Good sign. Da gods are wit you.

Snake eye intent is humungous
in wun unreal focus.

Looking through da slender blades
you size up da looming adversary.

Down in da green jungle carpet
dere's no kryptonite heah

to weaken da resolve.

Da stars are aligned
and perfectly centered

just like dat "S" tattooed on your head.

You no need wun red cape foa fly

wen you spring wun deadly surprise
wit two lethal fangs.

Da buggah nevah know
wat hit 'um

as wun fiery lava flow
surges through da veins—

Looks like Rikki-Tikki-Tavi
going bite da dust.

It's just anadah version
in wun multicolored dream

viewing da victory parade

and buzzing in da triumph
of wun mongoose killah.

CAPTAIN OF DIS FANTASY

Dere's wun crystal ball
in da Ala Wai Canal

stuck in da mud
undahneath wun school of tilapia.

It's part of da strange story
dat Chinky Barbarosa wen spin.

Like wun gypsy on magic mushrooms
he looked inside dat glass globe

and wrote down wat he saw.

In wun high-rise in Waikiki

wun infinite being
wit three heads and six hands

holding wun gun, his faddah,
and wun piece of toast,

looked outside da window
at da golf course below

and saw wun naked wahine
on top of wun blue rhinoceros

eating wun apple.

All of dis wuz interesting

but I taught da poetic twist
of da Holy Trinity wuz just too weird

and I told Chinky so.

He got offended

so he made da gun
shoot da faddah

and den he ate
da piece of toast.

I had to remind him
dat he wuz only wun character

wun figment of my creation

using my keyboard
to fill up my white space

but he nevah like listen.

I even suggested
dat wun giant serpent

might be bettah
den wun blue rhinoceros

but he just blew dat off.

He gave me lots of lip

and told me dat he could do
watevah he wanted to.

But wen he made da rhino
take wun crap on my shoes

while da naked wahine
gave me da middle fingah

I had enough—

I highlighted his story
hit delete

and da rebellion wuz ovah.

No moa tilapia
no moa Barbarosa

and no moa crystal ball
stuck in da mud.

SHAKA ATTACK

Okay
somebody got bit by wun shark again.

Ooooh— Big time news story!

Eidah dey dead
or dey just got away wit wun bad bite.

Shocking, aah? Humans.

Go out into da deep watah
wheah anyting could happen.

No get me wrong
I not telling you foa get paranoid.

I just letting you know
dat wats lurking dere in da depths

is not likely to be found
in your neighborhood swimming pool.

Brah, wen you go into da ocean
and dere's dis creature as big as your car

wit wun mouth full of sharp razors
and wun aggressive appetite

you just might be breakfast,
dinner, or lunch.

So if you like dangle your legs and feet
from wun surfboard and look like wun turtle

or go swimming freestyle
far beyond da reef

go for it—
just know dat you are not alone.

Moa bettah you flash wun shaka sign
to da horizon

as you look out ovah da surface of da watah.

If anyting
because of dat gesture

you can have comfort

in believing dat da gods,
God, fate, or watevah,

going keep your numbah
from coming up

in da big fish wit teeth lottery.

FISH FIGHT

All da fishermen stay fighting
cause no moa fish.

If you from "da gathering place"

no cross da Molokai Channel
to "da friendly isle"

cause dey going whack you
in da head wit wun bat.

If everyting stay
fished out off of Oahu

dats just too bad

cause da neighbor island boys
not going let you move in on dere turf.

Keep dat in mind
wen you approach da coastline

cause dey going follow you
all around da island.

Tings going get worse
I telling you—

You can trow
some Kaunakakai guys in jail

foa beating up
some guys from Heeia Kea

but da bad blood
not going go away.

Pretty soon

dey going start shooting bullets
on da high seas

and somebody going be sent down
to Davy Jones's Locker.

Oahu guys
wen deplete all of dere resources

and now dey like go Molokai
and take everyting ovah deah.

From Ilio Point to Laau Point

da locals stay looking out
ovah da watah at Oahu

wit wun simple kine message—

Moa bettah you eat
imported cod or can tuna

and leave our fishing grounds alone.

WEN DA BIRDS STOP SINGING

Da buggahs going be in da bushes
in da trees and in da grass—

dey going be everywheah
wit dere tongues flicking in da air.

Invasion, brah,
and big time change.

It happened before.

As wun mattah of fact
it's just like da arrival of da mosquito.

Da old time island people
nevah hear buzzing in dere ears

until wun American whaling ship
came to Lahaina in 1826

wit wun contaminated watah supply.

Paradise instantly
became wun paradise to da mosquito

and tink about all da new bodies
dey had to bite.

And not only dat

dose little blood suckers
wen affect all of da native birds too

because dey carry stuff like avian malaria.

Nowadays scientists worry

dat da surviving native birds
high up on da slopes

going eventually be attacked

by cold tolerant mosquitoes
dat going mutate ovah time.

Dey tinking
dat da last native birds going become extinct.

Unreal, aah?
How you like dat foa wun nightmare?

But you know wat?
Dey no need worry about da mosquitoes, brah,

because native birds or any adah kine birds
going be long gone

by da time dose tiny insects
reach da mountaintops—

da new invaders going make sure of dat.

Dese guys are coming by air
on military transports from Guam

and slowly dey are slithering off of da tarmac
and into da forest—

Say hello to da brown tree snake
and aloha to da mynah birds and doves.

It's not gonna be wun party

wen all of our feathery friends are gone
and scaly serpents stay all ovah da place.

Auwe!
Wat a bummah!

Mosquitoes and snakes in paradise
like plagues in ancient Egypt—

Wheah in da world is Moses
wen you need 'um?

KAKAAKO MACHO

If you like dense urban living
you going love Kakaako Macho.

Da future is on da doorstep, brah.

Yeeha! Buildings 700 feet tall!

Now da homeless
going have moa far to look up

while all da high makamakas wit bucks

going get 3 bedroom apartments
dat going be closah to da clouds.

Kakaako Macho—

solid like concrete
and strong like steel

to da developers dat going cash in
slippery like wun eel.

Cowabunga, brah!

Let's take da family on wun visit
and ride da new commuter train.

Going be like Chicago
witout da wind

and you going be able to view
all da coconut tree murals

painted on da towering walls.

Tokyo, Hong Kong, Shanghai,

say goodbye to da Hawaiian eye
dat could see mauka and makai.

Eh, look at da bird up dere
in da bright blue slits

in between da imposing
monolithic man-made gray—

da buggah is flying away.

HIDING DERE IN DA OCEAN GRASS

Da swimming cow
wen finish chewing her cud

and crazy sounds
wuz beginning to blare out of her ears

like wun strange alien jazz.

She looked to da horizon
as if she wuz looking foa answers

and saw wun big white whale

spouting wun response
in da shape of wun question mark.

Harpoons began rising from da depths
and shot into da sky

poking big kine holes
into da wings of jet fighters

dat wen go crashing one by one
into da seaside mountains.

Nearby all da bright red dolphins
starting jumping ovah da moon

as Captain Ahab
wuz sucking on wun large medicine spoon

cause wun huge tail flipper
wen whack him on da head.

Delirium wen swirl him
into wun iridescent whirlpool

twirling wit wun chorus of mad starfish
and angry sardines

dat screamed like sirens
all da way down

until da fever wen break
wen dey wen hit rock bottom.

Tossing in her bed in wun sweat

Janet nevah know
it could turn out dis way.

She taught she had wun bad flu

wen she wuz dealing
wit all of dose hallucinations.

Now she knows
it's not like da old days

wen Grandpa Toshi wen pick da stuff
fresh from da reef

and bring it home
to share wit da extended family.

So much foa da processed ogo

nicely packaged
dat she wen buy from da store.

Tainted on da production line
da plastic bag held wun unhealthy surprise

cause it wuz full of salmonella
hiding dere in da ocean grass.

OBSERVING DA OBSERVATORY

Da defense of Mauna Kea as sacred land
and da plans to build anadah telescope
on da mountaintop.

Dey looking at us through wun microscope

while some of us stay looking foa dem
through wun telescope.

It's da strangest ting
being someone else's paramecium.

Makes you wonder
if dey can see

da clash of science
and spirituality

in da cosmic petri dish.

We stay so tiny

dat our intellectual concepts
no show up.

Foa da guys wit big eyes
it's impossible to know

wat da micro creatures
are actually tinking.

Sacred or sacrilegious
progression or regression

it doesn't register
to dem

dat da observed life forms
dat dey stay looking at

are at odds
on wun island teardrop.

Dey no can hear
da pahu drum

way out deah beyond
beating like wun heartbeat.

Mauna Kea is just wun locale.

Part of da environment

foa da little bugs
to splash around in.

Big eye scientist
small eye scientist

looking up
or looking down

da buggahs are all da same.

Dey sticking
wit da analytical observations

failing to see
wun intuitive approach.

Protecting da sanctity of da land
or da realm of da supernatural

is so incomprehensible
to even consider or explore.

It's way moa foreign to dem
den da understanding of da universe.

POLYNESIAN HONG KONG

Choke human beings, brah,

like wun dog
wit five million fleas.

On dis island
it's wun good ting if you got money

adahwise

you going find yourself
on da down and out

living on da beach.

Meanwhile da tourists
fly into town

wit dere expensive cameras

expensive reservations

and expensive expectations
on da wonders of paradise.

Watching da jets land

you stay stuck in traffic
headed to your job

if you got one

tinking how
you going shuffle da bills

as you fall deeper into debt.

Choke budgets
choke people

choke stress

everybody choking
on da fear of choking.

Polynesian Hong Kong

it's wun hootenanny
and wun hoedown

if you stay on da top
and you pull da strings
on all da puppet clowns.

If not
just dangle dere in space

wit dat submissive look
on your face

and tink how wonderful
all of it used to be.

WHEAH DA HOMELESS WEN GO

Sanitize da sidewalks
sanitize da view

everyting nice and shiny
in da tourist mecca zoo

now Waikiki stay all wonderful
cause no moa any bums on da street.

If you stay homeless
and you lie down on da ground

pretty soon you not going be around

cause dey going slap you
wit wun fine you no can pay.

Dats wun novel way

of getting rid
of wat you no like see—

scare 'um out of town
or send dem off to jail

just foa being poor.

Give da cops wun scrub brush
and da city is sparkling clean

wit new rules
by da politicians

it's wun whole different scene.

Gaddah keep da tourists
spending dere money

in wun vagrant free zone

and make all da business guys happy.

So smile and say cheese

and snap your camera
in wun paradise unknown

as Waikiki gets wun facelift
to go wit its heart of stone.

PLAYING GOLF ON LOIHI

Dey wen land wun unmanned probe
on wun comet da adah day

and da scientific community
stay all giddy

proclaiming it's wun great step
for humankind

in understanding
da possible creation of our planet.

Same kine research hype

wen dey wen land guys on da moon
years earlier in 1968—

Da big chrome mega beast of progress
marches on

while all da common people
get passed by undah its feet.

Da nerds
at da space agency

cheer and shout
in dere bubble insulated jobs

as poverty remains rampant

all ovah da world.

So now dey like drill
into da surface of da comet

and analyze some dust and ice.

Moa bettah dey drill

into da surface
of da indifferent mind

and solve some of da problems
on earth first.

And wen do you tink
dat going happen you might ask?—

Long aftah
dey playing golf on Loihi

planning dere next project
at da nineteenth hole.

MOA SPACE FOA RAMBLE

Sell dat beachfront property now
and get as much as you can foa da house.

Wheah you got your plumeria tree
and nice green lawn

going be wun playground foa da fishes.

Methane from da tundra
and CO_2 from smoke stacks and exhaust pipes

going turn all dat melted ice from da poles
into moa watah foa da lobsters and da eels.

Middle of da island
dats da place to go.

Dere's no getting around it
cause da coastline going sink.

Take wun good look at da airport
and da brand new rail—

all of it is moving inland, brah.

Waikiki going be real different too.

Might as well just give it up
cause wun surrounding wall not going help.

Too bad no can build da same kine mega dam
dat dey going make in San Francisco Bay.

Da Golden Gate sure going look different.

Global warming—

Foa da longest time
plenty people wen blow it off as wun myth.

Now Kanaloa going have moa space foa ramble.

DA LAST SQUID

Willy Boy wen score.

On da mudflat
wheah da reef used to be

he wen speah da buggah—
da last squid, brah.

In da abandoned conservation area

between da industrial park
and da old desalinization plant

he wen find 'um

dough how any squid
could live ovah deah

I dunno.

Maybe da ting
wuz wun mutant, aah?

And as to how

Willy could go diving in dat spot
next to da effluent outflow

I dunno eidah.

You know wat "effluent" mean, aah?
Dats just wun nice word foa dodo watah.

But still den

Willy wuz all excited
aftah he wen cook dat squid.

Wen he wuz cutting 'um up
he wen tell me,

*"Eh, you know wat dis is, aah?
Dis is da last squid, braddah!"*

Da last squid—

It's kinnah funny, brah,
wen I tink back

but it really wuz da last squid.

Now by dat same beach
nutting can even live

cause da watah stay all black
and even moa polluted den before.

It's just like tings wen change ovahnight.

But you know
it started long time ago.

Way back wen

I remembah my maddah told me
just before I wuz born

dat dey wuz building wun second city on Oahu
and finishing wun new tunnel
on da windward side.

Latah on
wen I wuz growing up

tings wen accelerate

and da whole island
wen just develop out of control

into wun huge monstah city.

By den
had so many adah tunnels too

dat da mountain
wen look like wun honeycomb.

Everyting came different, brah,

cause da island
wen grow so fast

and had so many people.

Maybe good ting Willy Boy wen die early.

He nevah live to see
how tings got even moa worse.

But back den
wen we wuz youngah

he looked so happy
wen he wuz cutting up dat contaminated squid.

I can still hear his words—

"Dis is special, brah.
Dis is da last one."

Wen he wen offah me some

foa lottah reasons
dats hard foa explain

I just told 'um,

"Naah. No need."

But deep inside, brah,

I nevah like be da one to eat
da last squid.

DA BUGGAH IS GONZU

Da buggah is gonzu
in transit to da outtah zones

like wun departing astronaut
seeing how blue da marble really is.

He gazes down at da big bumboocha
and steers himself away.

Da buggah is gonzu

da rocket went vertical
and da laulau jumped ovah da moon.

Try look, try see,

up in da sky
it's wun incredibility!

Fastah den wun silver bullet

and able to leap da chasm
of time and space

he looks like wun ezy ridah wit wings
as he makes his way into da cosmos.

Echoing down wun starry corridor
at da speed of light

and leaving memory in its wake

he stay crossing wun grand frontier
razor sharp and super swift.

Now he stay behind da beyond
and foa sure everyone can agree

if you look around you going find
dat da buggah is gonzu.

ROADSIDE TURNOFF

Whipping and swirling paisley winds

wun voodoo blast
slammed into da eardrums like wun cyclone

as da ghost of Jimi Hendrix exhaled.

I walked into da run-down bar to see
wun poster of wun painting
by Hieronymus Bosch

hanging up on da wall.

The Garden of Earthy Delights

wuz viewed to wun psychedelic soundtrack
coming from wun old-fashioned jukebox—

It wuz wun peculiar synergy.

At da roadside turnoff

bikers and barflies
filled da watering hole next to wun gas station.

Outside tumbleweeds rambled
into da far reaches of da desert

like da slurred stories
from some of da patrons.

Most of dem
wuz hollowed out like dying cactus trees.

Dere wuz sand in my shoes
but clarity in my head.

I had stopped to ask foa directions.

Da bartender laughed

and cherry topped his answer
wit wun smirk

even dough it sounded
like wun familiar cliché—

*"Just keep driving east
on the highway," he said,*

"until you reach somewhere."

DEER JOHN—

I just wanted to let you know
I no live in Kailua anymoa.

Dat comes to mind
as I drive down Route 82

cause all da streets
stay lined wit shave ice foa miles.

It's January and it's cold too
and it's like living in wun white refrigerator—

frigid, brah!

Sometimes I figure moa bettah I punt
but no can.

I stay stuck heah
in dis freaking wintah wonderland.

Dats wat happens
wen you marry wun woman from Ohio.

Yeah, I tink about lots of tings

wen I stay driving down
Route 82 in da early evening

coming home aftah work.

Da last ting I taught
I would be tinking about dough

wuz my experience wit Deer John.

Dats wat I wen name him latah, brah.

He came right outtah da lights
of da oncoming traffic

cause he wuz trying to bolt across da road.

I nevah even see 'um until he wuz right deah
in da front of my car

and I wen hit 'um dead center!
It wuz just like driving into wun wall.

Aftah da collision
I wen look into my right side mirror

and saw wun big silhouette wit antlers

crumbling into wun heap
on da side of da road—

Great, I wen just kill Deer John.

I nevah feel too happy about dat
but suddenly I had adah problems to tink about

like da functionality of my car.

I noticed da front looked kinnah different

so I wen pull off of da road
to check out da situation.

Da impact wit Deer John
wen buckle da hood ovah da engine
on both sides

put wun crack in my left headlight

and left wun big dent
right deah on da front of my car.

I wuz all bum out at first

but den I wen tink
it could have been worse.

Good ting I wuz only doing 30.

If I wen hit dat buggah at 45
my car would have been toast!

Latah on I wen pound out da hood
wit wun rubbah mallet

and I got da side buckles out
so da ting could lay flat.

Den I wen put duct tape

ovah da crack in da left headlight.

I still had da big dent
right in da front of da hood

but you know wat?— so wat?

Da car is wun old Saturn
and at least it still runs.

It can get me to work
and dats da most important ting.

Yeah, I no stay in Kailua anymoa.

Ovah deah you not too likely
to hit wun big mountain pig in da road

dat going cause da same kine damage
as wun deer to your car.

If anyting
you going run ovah wun mongoose

and notice wun little bump undah your tire.

You might feel bad at first
but at least your car going be fine

and couple miles down da road
you going forget about it—

cause everybody in Hawai'i knows

you got too many of dose buggahs
running around anyway.

OPERA BY DA LAKE

Dere wuz wun comatose man.

Wun woman took him to Edgewater Park
and sat him in wun lawn chair.

Dark glasses and wun baseball cap
shielded his eyes from da sun.

Wun Frisbee came sailing
and hit him in da back of his head.

He woke up in amazement
to see wun flock of seagulls ovah da watah

and wondered wat happened
to all da mynah birds—

*It wuz just wun scene
in wun fleeting daydream.*

On wun bluff
not far from da Richard Wagner statue

dat same man looked out again at Lake Erie
and imagined da Pacific Ocean dis time

wit da Hawaiian Islands
somewheah beyond da horizon.

His stare wuzn't as frozen
as da eyes on da monument

but in some ways
it wuz just as displaced.

Da composer's memory wuz brought heah
by admiring German immigrants

who commissioned his image
to stand in perpetual observance.

He wuz wun long way from Bayreuth.

Da man gazing out ovah da lakeshore

wuz brought heah by wun Cleveland woman
who somehow became his wife.

He wuz wun long way from Wahiawa.

In wun opera dat only one man could hear
da rhythmic cadence of wun sharkskin drum

blended wit da performance
of wun orchestra in Berlin

as wun nearby train joined in
and rumbled its wheels upon da tracks.

MAFIOSO PIZZA

Soon aftah I wen move
into da new neighborhood

I walked around wun corner to see
wun catchy sign
above wun storefront window—

Mafioso Pizza.

Next to da name of da joint

wuz wun depiction
of wun 1930s Chicago style gangster.

Da character wuz wearing
wun fedora and wun suit

and he wuz smiling
while he wuz holding wun Tommy gun.

Da caption on da bottom of da sign read,
"There's no crime in killing your hunger."

One of my friends did tell me

dat dis West Side area wuz moa rougher
den wheah I used to live.

At least da owner of da pizzeria
had wun sense of humor.

Den again
it's not as crazy as da East Side of town.

Cleveland's police
and some bad guys dat just happened to be
black

recently took it
to wun new kine height ovah deah.

Law enforcement
responded to wun high speed car chase

by using wun bazooka to kill wun ant.

Five dozen cop cruisers
joined in on da intense pursuit

wen da fleeing car
tried to make its getaway.

Aftah da vehicle
wuz stopped and cornered
13 officers unloaded 137 bullets into da car.

One highly amped cop
jumped up on da hood

and fired rounds
point blank through da windshield.

It sounds exciting

but he wuz only putting extra holes
into two freshly snuffed out corpses.

Before he did dat

da people in da front seat
wuz already dead
from da preceding hail of gunfire.

Dere must be some deep reasons
on both sides

to ramp up da energy to dat extent.

Bottom line

it wuz just anadah day
in da big city wit big reactions

next to da big lake.

I guess I'll go home and turn on my TV
to find out wat going happen next—

Unless of course
I see it in person out on da streets.

BLUE DIAMOND

Pono looked at his hand
and spread his fingahs like wun fan.

Den he wen stare into his palm
at all da lifelines and fronds.

Dere wuz wun stirring in da breeze

and coconut leaves
wuz bending and refraining.

Pono wuz on wun different island now

as big as wun baseball mound
inside wun blue diamond.

Da ocean wuz just beyond
all da nicely cut angles.

He could see da currents moving
but he couldn't hear da sound

of all da people dat wuz circling around
in dere outriggah canoes.

Dey wuz calling like seabirds
looking almost like ghosts.

Outside da snow wuz falling

and wun squirrel
wuz jumping from wun branch.

Pono held his hand up to da light
coming in from da window

and it made wun fat silhouette
against wun calligraphy of bare trees.

Funny wat he wuz tinking about
wen he wuz tinking about home.

BITE DA EYE

Wen we wen buss out
wit all da local kine slang

da haoles at da adah tables

wen look at each of us
like we had two heads—

we might as well have been from Pluto.

Dey wuz listening
to two island expatriates

one from Ohio
and one from Michigan

talking wit da visitor from Hawai'i.

Da Pidgin flew like wun strange bird
in dat small breakfast café in Ann Arbor.

Wen da waitress wen bring da pancakes
dat wuz as big as da plate dey wuz on

da island vernacular wen flap its wings.

"Ho, dose buggahs are huge!"

And wen she wen arrive
wit my order of hash browns, eggs, and ham

I wen say aftah I wen try 'um,

"Ono kine grinds, brah,
and da ham not dat salty!"

We wuz talking story
in dat same familiar language

about da place
wheah we wen all grow up.

Anykine stuff

from spearfishing and bodysurfing
to da secrets of catching squid.

"Yeah, brah,

you bite da eye
and den you turn da squid head inside out."

Wun haole lady
at wun nearby table heard dat

and she had wun look on her face
like she wuz tinking,

"What the hell are these people
talking about?"

It shall remain wun mystery to her

cause we wen bite da eye
and we wen also bite da ears.

PINCHPENNY MODE

I don't know how I got heah
but heah I am

counting how many pinto beans
I put into my potato soup.

Pinchpenny mode—

So dis is wat dey call
wun "fixed budget."

Aftah da rent, electric bill,
phone bill, and food expenses,

I just cleah da monthly hurdle
by da skin of my okole.

Anyting else happen
I stay in da red.

Imagine wun anorexic Santa Claus
holding wun empty bag—

Dats me, braddah.

One foot from da grave

and anadah one from sleeping
on da sidewalk.

At least I got wun good dose
of indifference

to get me through da day.

And too bad dese penny coins
wuzn't golden doubloons instead—

Den I wouldn't have to pinch myself
to remind me dat I still stay heah.

NOT DAT BIG OF WUN DROP

I no remembah
doing any cartwheels wen I found out.

It's like anyting else
wen your optimism takes wun nosedive—

Howevah, you do find
dat disappointment beats apathy

cause going from terrible to horrible
is not dat big of wun drop.

Eh, you can be forceful if you like

and make wun full on samurai charge
wit your sword gleaming in da sun

but wen da machine guns mow you down
aftah you stand up to attack

you going find out fast
how it really is.

I no like sound like wun killjoy

but sometimes life is as tough
as wun 50 cent steak.

So now you telling me
about all da silver linings in da clouds

and all da bluebirds of happiness
singing in da trees.

Excuse me
if I no get carried away

and start swooning
to da glitter and da fairy dust.

I've kicked plenty tires
and seen tons of flats.

Eventually
you get to da point

wheah you see
da genuine landscape.

Dis isn't someting
on da way to someting else—

Dis is it.

BUG IN WUN JAR

All da young girls and guys
dat going sprout wen I stay gone

I'm leaving stuff foa you
cause I going have to hele on.

Dis physical body dat I'm wearing
stay living in da final chapter.

So dey going collect up all my words
and dey going tell you wat I mean

da professors and da scholars
and da literary machine

watevah it is
it's just wun observation to me.

I had fun wen I did it
it wuz catharsis to da brain

and wat you reading right now
is da spark dat still remains

just anadah poetic fling
added to da whole collection.

Maybe it's wun honor
to be studied from afar

to be pondered
and examined

like wun bug in wun jar—

Academia going do
wat dey going do.

Because of dat

I'll offer wun compiled exoskeleton
foa da eggheads to dissect.

Meanwhile
my advice to da girls and guys

wen dey read wat I wen write—

"Da eyes going see
wat da eyes going see

da ears going listen
and da spirit going be free."

Incidentally

I going be loving
my new translucent body

cause wen I spread my wings
I going fly right through da glass.

Acknowledgements

Poems in this book have previously appeared in *Otoliths, Chaminade Literary Review, Unlikely Stories Mark V, Hawai'i Review, Eskimo Pie, Kaimana—Literary Arts Hawai'i, Mad Swirl, Aloha 'Āina Zine: In Solidarity with Mauna Kea, Angry Old Man, Misfit Magazine, The Lake, 'Ōiwi—A Native Hawaiian Journal, Yellow Mama, Futures Trading, The City Poetry, Snorkel, Synchronized Chaos, The Rising Phoenix Review, Juked, Tinfish, In Between Hangovers, Beautiful Losers Magazine, I am not a silent poet, Bamboo Ridge, Eleventh Transmission, Rasputin: A Poetry Thread, Whetu Moana: Contemporary Polynesian Poems in English, Modern Poetry Quarterly Review, Dead Snakes, Hawai'i Pacific Review,* and *The Curly Mind.*

CPSIA information can be obtained
at www.ICGtesting.com
Printed in the USA
LVHW052212020522
717804LV00004B/237